AN ILLUSTRATED DICTIONARY OF
SAINTS

A guide to the lives and works of over 180 of the
world's most notable saints, with expert commentary
and more than 350 beautiful llustrations

BY TESSA PAUL
CONSULTANT REVEREND RONALD CREIGHTON-JOBE

southwater

This edition is published by Southwater,
an imprint of Anness Publishing Ltd,
Blaby Road,
Wigston,
Leicestershire
LE18 4SE
info@anness.com
www.southwaterbooks.com;
www.annesspublishing.com

Anness Publishing has a new picture agency
outlet for images for publishing, promotions
or advertising. Please visit our website
www.practicalpictures.com for more
information.

Publisher: Joanna Lorenz
Editorial Director: Helen Sudell
Executive Editor: Joanne Rippin
Designer: Elizabeth Healey
Jacket design: Adelle Morris
Picture Researcher: Debra Weatherley
Production Controller: Bessie Bai

ETHICAL TRADING POLICY

At Anness Publishing we believe that business
should be conducted in an ethical and
ecologically sustainable way, with respect
for the environment and a proper regard to
the replacement of the natural resources
we employ.

As a publisher, we use a lot of wood pulp in
high-quality paper for printing, and that wood
commonly comes from spruce trees. We are
therefore currently growing more than
750,000 trees in three Scottish forest plantations: Berrymoss (130 hectares/320 acres),
West Touxhill (125 hectares/305 acres) and
Deveron Forest (75 hectares/185 acres). The
forests we manage contain more than 3.5
times the number of trees employed each
year in the books we manufacture.

Because of this ongoing ecological invest-
ment programme, you, as our customer, can
have the pleasure and reassurance of knowing
that a tree is being cultivated on your behalf
to naturally replace the materials used to make
the book you are holding. Our forestry
programme is run in accordance with the UK
Woodland Assurance Scheme (UKWAS) and
will be certified by the internationally
recognized Forest Stewardship Council (FSC).
The FSC is a non-government organization
dedicated to promoting responsible
management of the world's forests.
Certification ensures forests are managed in
an environmentally sustainable and socially
responsible way.

For further information about this scheme,
go to www.annesspublishing.com/trees

PUBLISHER'S NOTE

Although the advice and information in this
book are believed to be accurate and true at
the time of going to press, neither the
authors nor the publisher can accept any legal
responsibility or liability for any errors or
omissions that may be made.

Previously published as part of a larger
volume, *The Illustrated World Encyclopedia of Saints*

CONTENTS

INTRODUCTION

In the early years of the Church the meaning of the word "saint" was applied to all those who followed the teaching of Christ. As Christianity spread, however, it began to be applied to some Christians who lived lives of extraordinary faith. These people were held up to be eminent examples of moral virtue and were venerated after their deaths by the members of their local church. Eventually, the Church created a process through which such venerable people could be recognized as saints by all Christians everywhere.

During the long and complex history of canonization – the process of being recognized as a saint – sainthood has been invested with many different meanings. However, many characteristics are agreed upon. Whether a saint devotes their life to God, or demonstrates their holiness in secular life, they must be a person of great faith and religious devotion. A saint can be born to grace, or a reformed character, but whatever path their life has traced, they must show certain characteristics that make them "heroic", such as piety, fortitude, humility and courage.

Having been awarded a privileged place in heaven, saints are thought to be close to God and this closeness, combined with their humanity, makes them intermediaries that the faithful can turn to in times of need.

Above St George is the patron saint of England and many churches bear his name. In 1914, together with St John Chrysostom and St Roch, St George was declared a patron of Istanbul (Paolo Uccello, c.1439–40).

The wide range of people who have achieved sainthood is fascinating, for this special company does not recognize wealth, social status or professional achievement, and thus the canon includes peasants, nobles and kings. It also includes angels, and legends whose historical roots are lost in the mists of time, such as St George, St Christopher, and St Nicholas of Myra.

Many saints have been forgotten over time, while thousands of names are obscure or absent from historical record. There are more than 4,000 saints in the Roman Catholic canon and the selection made here is not intended to be comprehensive or exclusive. Instead, its purpose is to show that while all Christian saints are identical in their devotion to God, each one has their own talent and personality, and their own story of struggle.

This book tells the history of sainthood through the biographies of selected saints, listed in chronological order, while beautiful illustrations throughout show how these saints have been represented in art.

Right The Wilton Diptych *(right wing) showing the Madonna and angels (French School, c.1395).*

ARCHANGEL RAPHAEL

THIS ARCHANGEL IS THE HERO OF A LEGEND IN WHICH HE HELPS A POOR, BLIND MAN. HIS NAME MEANS "GOD HEALS", AND HE IS TRADITIONALLY SEEN AS BOTH A HEALER AND PROTECTOR.

Above Tobias and the Angel
(Andrea del Verrocchio, c. 1470–80).

The Gospel of John tells us that in Jerusalem there was once a pool called Bethesda where, at a certain time every year, "an angel" stirred its waters. The first people to enter the pool after this visit would be cured of their illness or disability. By tradition, Raphael is credited as this very angel.

In the Apocryphal Book of Tobit, there are many stories about Raphael. Disguised as a man, he takes a journey with a boy, Tobias, and his dog. They travel to recover a debt owed to the boy's blind grandfather, and have many adventures. On their return home, Raphael restores the old man's sight by asking him to eat a particular fish. Most paintings of this archangel show him with a fish, the boy and the dog, and he is a patron of travellers.

KEY FACTS

Divine messenger of God
DATES: *Not human but a manifestation of God*
PATRON OF: *Travellers, young people leaving home, sad people, health inspectors, the sick, the blind and against eye disease*
FEAST DAY: *29 September*
EMBLEM: *Holding a bottle, carrying a fish or a staff, accompanied by a boy*

ARCHANGEL MICHAEL

THE ARCHANGEL MICHAEL SAVED HEAVEN BY VANQUISHING THE DEVIL WHO WAS INTRUDING WHILE DISGUISED AS A DRAGON.

Above The Archangel Michael Defeating Satan *(Guido Reni, c. 1600–42).*

The Old Testament describes Michael as the protector of Israel, "always interceding for the human race". He was the angel who spoke to Moses on Mount Sinai. The New Testament says he "has authority over the people" and "gave them the law".

Archangel Michael fought the Devil when war broke out in heaven. Michael defeated the beast and the angels siding with it, so he was given the right to judge souls seeking entry into heaven.

Many medieval images show Michael weighing human souls brought before him for judgement. He is very often pictured fighting the dragon. Michael is the patron of battles and soldiers, as well as those believed to be "possessed by the devil".

Archangel Michael appeared in visions at Monte Gargano in Apulia, Italy, in the 5th century AD. Many churches worldwide, especially those built on hilltops, are dedicated to him, such as Mont-St-Michel in France.

KEY FACTS

Divine messenger of God
DATES: *Not human but a manifestation of God*
PATRON OF: *Ambulance drivers, bakers, mariners, paramedics, soldiers and battles*
FEAST DAY: *29 September*
EMBLEM: *Frequently dressed in armour carrying a gatekeeper's staff, sword, scales, banner, dragon*

ARCHANGEL GABRIEL

THE ARCHANGEL GABRIEL DELIVERS SOME OF GOD'S MOST IMPORTANT MESSAGES TO MAN. HE INFORMED BOTH ELIZABETH AND MARY THAT THEY WOULD SOON GIVE BIRTH.

In the Old Testament, Gabriel was present at the burial of Moses and at an Israelite victory over the Assyrians. He visited the prophet Daniel to warn him of the coming of the Messiah, saviour of the Israelites. He also helped Daniel interpret a dream that rescued the Israelites.

In the New Testament, the Archangel Gabriel was charged with telling Zachary that his wife Elizabeth would bear a son who would play an important role in the Messiah's life. This son was John the Baptist.

THE ANNUNCIATION

The most important message Gabriel delivered was to the Virgin Mary. He appeared before her to announce she had been chosen, above all women, to give birth to Jesus, the Son of God. His greeting to Mary, reported in the Gospel of Luke, has become the start of the "Hail Mary".

The Annunciation, Gabriel's visitation to the Virgin Mary, has been the subject of hundreds of paintings. The archangel always has wings and often wears a courtier's clothes, or a white tunic covered by a cloak.

Some traditions hold that, accompanied by "a multitude of heavenly hosts", Gabriel appeared above the hills of Bethlehem where shepherds were tending their flock. He announced the birth of Jesus to them.

In an ancient chapel on the Appian Way in Rome there is an early image of Gabriel. Some medieval depictions show him carrying the staff of a doorkeeper to show that he is a guardian of the Church.

His feast day used to be 24 March, date of the Annunciation. In 1969, the pope decided he should share a feast day with archangels Michael and Raphael.

Below *The Archangel Gabriel appears before Mary for the* Annunciation *(Sandro Botticelli, c. 1489–90).*

"Hail Mary, full of grace.
The Lord is with thee.
Blessed art thou amongst women,
and blessed is the fruit of thy womb, Jesus.
Holy Mary, Mother of God,
pray for us sinners, now and at the hour
of our death."

GABRIEL'S GREETING TO MARY MAKES UP THE FIRST TWO LINES OF THE "HAIL MARY" PRAYER

MARY, THE VIRGIN

MARY IS THE UNIVERSAL SYMBOL OF PURITY AND MOTHERHOOD. MANY CHRISTIANS BELIEVE SHE WAS FREE OF SIN FROM THE MOMENT SHE WAS CONCEIVED, A DOCTRINE KNOWN AS THE IMMACULATE CONCEPTION.

KEY FACTS
*Mother of the
Son of God*
DATES: *1st century BC*
BIRTH PLACE: *Unknown*
PATRON OF: *Motherhood,
virginity*
FEAST DAY: *15 August*
EMBLEM: *Blue robes, crown, lily*

The image of Mary, the Blessed Virgin, is instantly recognizable, whether as a mother with her child in her arms or with her dead son laid across her lap. A mother nurtures her child, and her suffering for the sake of that child is intense. Mary, in the role of the Holy Mother, represents feelings understood by everyone. No saint can match the mother of the Son of God.

EARLY LIFE

Little is known about Mary's early life. There are no dates for her birth or her death, and mention of her parents Anne and Joachim is only found in the apocryphal 2nd-century AD Gospel of James.

We do know, from the Bible, that the Blessed Virgin was a young Jewish girl, and that like her future husband Joseph, she was said to be descended from the family of the great Israelite king, David.

MOTHER OF CHRIST

It was the angel Gabriel who told Mary that she was to be the mother of Christ, an event known as the Annunciation. The angel said that the child would be

Left Mary and the baby Jesus are depicted as playful and loving in this stained glass from Eaton Bishop, England (14th century).

by animals. Shepherds and later three wise men, the Magi, came to worship the young Messiah.

After the Nativity, Mary is mentioned only a few times in the gospels. Mary and Joseph took Jesus for his presentation at the Temple of Jerusalem, as was the custom. With Joseph and Jesus she fled to Egypt to save their child from slaughter by Herod's men. At the marriage feast at Canaan, Mary asked Jesus to intervene when the wine ran out. And when Jesus hung dying on the cross, Mary kept vigil close by.

The Blessed Virgin was also with the apostles at Pentecost, the time after Christ's Ascension when the Holy Spirit is believed to have descended upon them. There is no mention of Mary living with Jesus and his apostles or teaching during this time.

Left A sculpture of Mary cradling the body of her dead son (I. Günther, 18th century). Artistic images of this moment are known as "the Pietà".

the Son of God, not of a man. Mary accepted this extraordinary fate with great faith and courage.

The Roman population census obliged Mary and Joseph to travel to the home of their ancestor, David. Mary gave birth to Jesus in a stable in Bethlehem, surrounded

LEVELS OF VENERATION

Mary, the Mother of God, is universally admired by Catholic believers. The Catholic Church accords different levels of honour. The highest level is adoration, or latria, and is reserved for God and the Trinity (God the Father, God the Son and God the Holy Ghost). Veneration of the Blessed Virgin is granted the Church's second highest honour and is known as hyperdulia, as theorized by Thomas Aquinas. Veneration of the company of all other saints is known as dulia.

were generally richly decorated with gold. They were portrayed as formal, grand and majestic.

Images from the late medieval and early Renaissance periods show a tender young woman with a baby. She is often clothed in a heavenly blue gown and the child is naked. Images of the Virgin Mary in the developing world more recently often show her dressed in the most admired style of the local people.

In today's Catholic and Orthodox worlds, Mary is still remembered when many other saints are neglected. Holy icons and festivals held in Mary's honour continue to attract millions of believers across the globe.

Above A detail from Wedding at Canaan, *the occasion when Jesus performed his first miracle by turning water into wine at the request of Mary (Paolo Veronese, 1563).*

A MOTHER'S PLACE

Although nothing is known of Mary's death, members of the Roman Catholic and Eastern Orthodox Churches hold that she was lifted body and soul into heaven. This event is celebrated as the Assumption. Her role as the mother of Jesus placed her very close to God in heaven.

Many believers think that if a person asks Mary to intercede on their behalf, her great influence is bound to bring God's forgiveness and redemption of their sins.

MARY IN ART

In earlier times Mary's image could be seen widely throughout Christendom. During the early medieval era, depictions of the Virgin Mary and the infant Jesus

Right Mary with the twelve apostles and two archangels in a Russian icon showing The Ascension *(c. 1450).*

JOSEPH

THRUST INTO THE UNIQUE ROLE OF EARTHLY FATHER TO THE SON OF GOD, JOSEPH PROVED A KINDLY HUSBAND AND CARING PARENT. HE PROTECTED HIS YOUNG FAMILY BY FLEEING FROM KING HEROD.

Joseph, husband of the Virgin Mary, was a godly man. He is most often portrayed as both honourable and compassionate.

He makes few appearances in the New Testament. The Gospels of both Mark and Luke describe his royal descent from the House of David, although a carpenter by trade. According to the Jewish prophets, the Messiah would come from this House.

Joseph's age is unknown. As the betrothed of a young woman, it may be fair to assume he was also relatively young at the time of his engagement. An indication of his noble character is given by the nature of his reaction when he learned Mary was pregnant. Not wishing to shame her, he decided to end the betrothal quietly. His distress was dispelled when an angel appeared and explained the intervention of the Holy Spirit.

THE FLIGHT INTO EGYPT

After the Nativity and the visit of the Magi, an angel interpreted one of Joseph's dreams, warning

KEY FACTS
Husband of the Virgin Mary
DATES: *1st century BC*
BIRTH PLACE: *Palestine*
PATRON OF: *Canada, Peru and Mexico, families, fathers, manual workers (especially carpenters), the homeless, exiles, travellers*
FEAST DAY: *19 March and 1 May*
EMBLEM: *Bible, branch, carpenter's tools, ladder, lamb, lily*

him of Herod's order to murder all the small boys in Bethlehem. This led Joseph to flee his home to save his wife and the baby Jesus. Numerous paintings depict Joseph as very protective of his family.

Later in Egypt, an angel let Joseph know when it was safe to return to Palestine, and he settled in Nazareth. He followed Jewish custom when he took his wife to the purification ceremony that all women underwent after giving birth. The scribes do not record Joseph's death but it is assumed he died sometime before the crucifixion of Jesus, as Joseph is not mentioned as present on this day.

OTHER INTERPRETATIONS

Joseph's actions show him worthy of his role as protector of the Son of God. Despite this, some apocryphal writings represent him as an old man and parent of other children. The travelling players of medieval theatre liked to present him as a clownish old fool.

Veneration for Joseph grew, however, and in 1870 he was declared patron of the Roman Catholic Church. A special day, 1 May, was dedicated to him as patron of manual workers.

Left A small angel reassures Joseph in The Doubt of St Joseph *(French School, c. 1410–20).*

ANNE

THE MOTHER OF THE BLESSED VIRGIN IS NOT MENTIONED IN THE CANONICAL GOSPELS, BUT APOCRYPHAL SOURCES PRAISE HER AND SHE HAS A LOYAL FOLLOWING NONETHELESS.

KEY FACTS

Mother of the Virgin Mary
DATES: *1st century* BC
BIRTH PLACE: *Unknown*
PATRON OF: *Childless women, horsemen and miners*
FEAST DAY: *26 July (West)*
EMBLEM: *Basket, door*

There is no firm evidence to determine the parentage or place of origin of the mother of the Virgin Mary. Yet believers longed to have information about the earthly grandmother of Jesus. There is an apocryphal text, the Gospel of James, that mentions her as a saint. Gregory of Nyssa, the brother of St Basil the Great and a saint in his own right, also refers to her with reverence.

In the Gospel of James, Anne is described as childless, and she "mourned in two mournings, and lamented in two lamentations". Her desperate prayers were answered when an angel visited her house to tell her she would bear a child.

Anne responded with the words, "As the Lord my God liveth, if I beget either male or female I will bring it as a gift to the Lord my God; and it shall minister to Him in holy things all the days of its life." So the Virgin Mary was consecrated to God even before her birth.

In the *Golden Legend*, stories of the saints from the 13th century, Anne's husband Joachim dies shortly after the birth of Mary. Anne remarries twice. She has a daughter by each of these new husbands, and both these girls are given the name of Mary. The girls grow up to produce many cousins for Jesus and two boy cousins become apostles. Despite the fictitious nature of both these sources, Anne became sufficiently important in the Church for her relics to appear at the church of Santa Maria Antiqua in Rome.

Above A young Mary is shown reading to her mother in this manuscript drawing (15th century).

Below The story of Mary's birth is here imagined within a contemporary Venetian domestic setting (Vittore Carpaccio, 1504–8).

LATER INFLUENCE

The figure of Anne remained in the public mind and artists favoured her as a subject. Paintings and stained glass illustrations show Anne as a tender mother to her little girl. Other images depict Anne teaching Mary how to weave and read.

An unexpected cultus grew in Constantinople (Istanbul) during the 6th century AD when Emperor Justinian I dedicated a shrine to St Anne. She was venerated in Europe from the 13th century. When England's King Richard II (1367–1400) married Anne of Bohemia in 1382, the English bishops petitioned the pope to grant a feast day for St Anne. Later, the official status of such an unsubstantiated figure aroused great anger in Martin Luther.

JOACHIM

JOACHIM IS HONOURED AS THE HUSBAND OF ANNE AND THE FATHER
OF MARY. HIS POPULARITY GREW IN THE WEST IN THE MIDDLE
AGES AS THE CULTUS OF THE BLESSED VIRGIN FLOURISHED.

KEY FACTS
Father of the Virgin Mary
DATES: *1st century* BC
BIRTH PLACE: *Unknown*
PATRON OF: *Fathers, grandfathers*
FEAST DAY: *26 July (West)*
EMBLEM: *Elderly man holding
doves, lamb*

This man became a saint by
virtue of being the husband
of St Anne and the father of the
Blessed Virgin. In Hebrew, his
name means "the Lord will
judge". The sources of information for him are entirely fictitious,
as they are for his wife.

In the *Golden Legend*, Joachim
is given a picturesque history. This
book tells how he was expelled
from the Jewish temple because,
after 20 years of marriage, he and
his wife remained childless.

Desolate and believing God
had cursed him, Joachim went to
seek refuge with a band of
shepherds. He decided to fast for
40 days. An angel visited and
comforted him with the news
that his wife would bear a child.
Excited, Joachim hurried home.

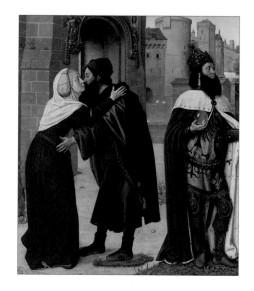

Above Charlemagne, and the
Meeting of Saints Joachim and
Anne at the Golden Gate
(the Master of Moulins, c.1500).

Below right Presentation of the
Virgin at the Temple *(Philippe de
Champaigne, 1639–40). Mary would
have been taken to a synagogue, but
this image depicts a Christian setting.*

But Anne, his worried wife,
was wandering through Jerusalem
looking for her husband. An angel
appeared and advised her to go to
the Golden Gate. There, Anne
found her husband. After this
happy reunion, she conceived the
child who would become the
Mother of God.

LATER RECOGNITION
The cultus of St Joachim began in
the East and was more popular
there than in the west. For several
centuries the Eastern Orthodox
Church has celebrated his feast day
on 9 September. The Roman
Catholic Church was less eager to
grant him sainthood, but the large
cultus could not be ignored. Pope
Gregory XV (1554–1623) allowed
him status as a saint, and Joachim
shares a feast day with his wife.

*Below left A fresco scene showing
Joachim among the shepherds (Giotto
di Bondone, c.1303–10).*

ELIZABETH

ELIZABETH WAS ELDERLY AND GENERALLY ASSUMED TO BE BARREN
WHEN SHE BECAME PREGNANT WITH THE BOY WHO WOULD BECOME
JOHN THE BAPTIST. THE ARCHANGEL GABRIEL DELIVERED THE NEWS.

KEY FACTS
*Wife of Zachary,
mother of John the Baptist*
DATES: *1st century BC*
BIRTH PLACE: *Probably Palestine*
PATRON OF: *Pregnancy*
FEAST DAY: *5 November*
EMBLEM: *Elderly woman*

It is assumed that Elizabeth was close to menopause when Gabriel announced that she was carrying a child. She was known to be childless, and the news must have brought her great joy.

Elizabeth, a descendant of the patriarch Aaron, is said to have been related to the Blessed Virgin. Their friendship was cemented by their fates as well as by blood.

Numerous paintings show these women together. Elizabeth was the first person to recognize Mary as the mother of the future Lord.

Left A detail of St Elizabeth from the church of Santa Maria di Porto Fuori, Italy (Ercole de' Roberti, c.1480–81).

ZACHARY

INITIALLY DOUBTFUL, ZACHARY
WAS JOYFUL AT THE PROMISE OF
A CHILD AND NAMED HIM JOHN.

The father of John the Baptist was a Jewish priest. He and his wife Elizabeth had long been married, but had no children.

Zachary was visited by the archangel Gabriel in the temple in Jerusalem, who announced that Elizabeth was to give birth to a child who would "make ready a people prepared for the Lord". Zachary doubted the words of the angel and was struck dumb.

At the baby's circumcision Elizabeth insisted that he was to be called John, going against the Jewish tradition that a child should be given a family name. Zachary supported her by writing on a tablet, "His name is John". Immediately, he regained his voice and began praising God. His words, known as the Benedictus, form part of the Church liturgy.

KEY FACTS
Father of John the Baptist
DATES: *1st century BC*
BIRTH PLACE: *Probably Palestine*
FEAST DAY: *5 November*

"And thou, O child, shall be called the prophet of the Most High; for thou shalt go before the Lord to prepare His ways, To give His people knowledge of salvation through forgiveness of their sins..."

THE BENEDICTUS
(CANTICLE OF
ZACHARY)

Left In this Flemish early Renaissance painting, Zachary is displayed in the fine clothes of a medieval baron to indicate his high status as the father of John the Baptist (Jan Provost, 1510).

JOHN THE BAPTIST

JOHN THE BAPTIST DEVOTED HIS LIFE TO WARNING PEOPLE TO "REPENT, FOR THE KINGDOM OF GOD IS AT HAND". HE DECLARED THAT THE MESSIAH WOULD SOON APPEAR AMONG THEM.

KEY FACTS
Baptized Jesus
DATES: *d.c.AD 30*
BIRTH PLACE: *Nazareth*
PATRON OF: *Pilgrims to the Holy Land, Knights Hospitallers, hoteliers, birdwatchers*
FEAST DAY: *24 June, 29 August*
EMBLEM: *Lamb, cross, a scroll*

The writings of Sts Jerome and Augustine of Hippo suggested that John the Baptist was sanctified in the womb and never committed a sin. He certainly chose a "heroic" life of hardship and poverty, dressing only in animal skins and living on food he could scavenge.

John devoted his life to telling people to prepare for the coming of the Messiah and his Kingdom.

He must have had a charismatic personality with great energy and determination, for he attracted a large following.

BY THE JORDAN

His youth was spent as a hermit, surviving on a diet of locusts and wild honey, a lifestyle that closely resembled that of some of the prophets of the Old Testament.

Crowds came to hear him preach, and John began to baptize them by dipping them in the River Jordan. When Jesus came through the crowd, a dove hovered over his head.

John took this bird to be a sign of the Holy Spirit, so he knew Jesus was the Messiah. He then baptized Jesus, saying he was "the Lamb of God who takest away the sins of the world". In paintings, John is often shown pointing at a lamb and holding a cross.

John the Baptist was later put in prison for denouncing an incestuous marriage between the governor of Galilee, Herod Antipas, and his niece, Herodias. His stepdaughter, Salome, pleased Herod so much with her dancing that he offered her anything she wanted. At her mother's prompting, the girl requested the head of John the Baptist. It was delivered to her on a platter.

TEACHINGS

The teachings of John the Baptist prepared the way for the work of Jesus. John preached about the presence of a "messianic kingdom" and the need for all to repent their sins. His lessons were

Left St John the Baptist in the Wilderness *(Hieronymus Bosch, c.1504–5). John the Baptist is shown in a landscape of strange plants with a lamb, one of his emblems.*

rooted in the Jewish belief that one day the Almighty would send a messiah to lead the people to righteousness. Many Jews who heard John speak were therefore sympathetic to the arrival of Jesus and accepted him as their long-awaited leader.

A large number of disciples followed John and imitated his severe ascetic mode of life. He taught them methods of prayer and meditation. Many ordinary, humble families were moved by his message, too.

Historians believe that John the Baptist's wanderings took him to the Dead Sea. Lessons similar to his message are recorded in the Dead Sea Scrolls – papyrus writings dating from the early Christian era. In Samaria, there is evidence of a community, the Mandaeans, or Sabaeans, who defined themselves as "Christians according to John". It seems these people preserved ideas and traditions that confused John the Baptist with Jesus.

Below Salome with the Head of Saint John the Baptist *(Bernardino Luini, c.1525–30). Salome is shown as a young woman with a sly and cunning expression.*

Left Saint John the Baptist *(Titian, c.1540). John may be dressed in skins and rags, but he is here presented as a powerful man and leader. The lamb lies at his feet.*

Medieval Christians prayed to John the Baptist, believing that through him, Christ would enter their souls. He is reputedly buried in Sebaste, Samaria. Alone among the saints, his feast day is held on his birthday. However, the date of his death is also celebrated in the West on 29 August.

An important saint, some of his relics are claimed to be held in St Sylvester's Church in Rome, and in Amiens, France. Many churches in Britain and Europe have been dedicated to him.

THE MEANING OF BAPTISM

Baptism is a religious purification ceremony in which a person is either immersed in water, or has water poured over their head. Baptism is part of the Christian tradition, but can be seen to have a precursor in the Jewish tradition of undergoing a *mikvah*, or cleansing ritual, for instance on conversion to Judaism.

Baptism has been subject to many interpretations by different Christian churches, and as a result has varied meanings. It can be seen as a path to salvation and a process by which a person is cleansed of their sins. In this way, baptism may help a convert to Christianity put their past behind them and start afresh.

Similarly, baptism may be seen as a symbolic death and rebirth, an interpretation put forward in the Bible by Paul who says that we share in the death, burial and rebirth of Jesus Christ through baptism. Baptism can also function as a symbol of conversion, through which a believer declares their faith and their membership of a particular church.

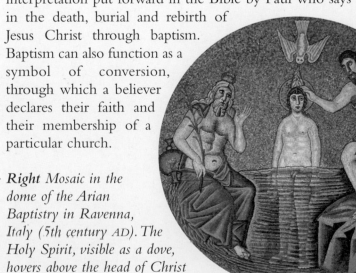

Right Mosaic in the dome of the Arian Baptistry in Ravenna, Italy (5th century AD). The Holy Spirit, visible as a dove, hovers above the head of Christ during his baptism by John.

DISMAS

JESUS COMFORTED DISMAS, THE "GOOD THIEF", AS TOGETHER THEY SUFFERED DEATH BY CRUCIFIXION. DISMAS FELT THAT UNLIKE JESUS HE DESERVED HIS PUNISHMENT AS HE HAD COMMITTED A CRIME.

KEY FACTS
Crucified next to Christ
DATES: *d.c.AD 30*
BIRTH PLACE: *Probably Galilee*
PATRON OF: *Thieves, condemned criminals, undertakers*
FEAST DAY: *25 March*
EMBLEM: *Tall cross, naked on cross*

Dismas, a common thief, was nailed to a cross next to Jesus on the day of the Crucifixion and spoke with him. The Eastern Orthodox Church has put in their litany the words that Dismas uttered to Jesus, "Lord," he said, "remember me when you come into your kingdom". Jesus gave the reassuring answer, "Today thou shalt be with me in Paradise".

Luke records the story in his gospel. Dismas reprimands the other thief, Gestas, who asks Jesus, as the Messiah, to prove it and save all three of them from death. According to a medieval story, some time previously, Dismas, in awe of the infant Jesus, had even ordered his fellow bandits to leave the Holy Family unmolested as they made their escape to Egypt.

In the Middle Ages, Dismas came to be seen as the patron saint of prisoners and thieves.

Right The Crucifixion *(Francesco Botticini, c.1471).*

VERONICA

AN ORDINARY WOMAN WITH A KIND HEART TRIED TO SOOTHE CHRIST AS HE CARRIED HIS CROSS ON THE WAY TO HIS CRUCIFIXION AT CALVARY. THE VEIL SHE USED BECAME AN IMPORTANT RELIC.

KEY FACTS
Wiped the brow of Christ
DATES: *1st century AD*
BIRTH PLACE: *Probably Galilee*
FEAST DAY: *12 July*
EMBLEM: *Veil with Christ's image upon it*

There is a strong possibility that Veronica is a legendary figure. Even her name is likely to be a combination of *vera*, meaning "true" in Latin, and *icon*, meaning "image" in ancient Greek. However, she figures in the Stations of the Cross, the 14 events that mark the journey of Christ carrying his cross to the Hill of Calvary.

Veronica was a woman in the mob who followed Jesus on his last earthly trip. The crowds pushed and shoved to catch a glimpse of this man, the so-called "King of the Jews", and many yelled insults in bloodthirsty tones. But scattered among the crowds were frightened, anxious and distressed Christians. Veronica was one of these. Pitying Jesus as he sweated and struggled under his burden, she took off her veil and wiped his brow.

An imprint of his face was left on the veil and it was taken to St Peter's Basilica in Rome in the 8th century. The veil became a popular relic in the 14th and 15th centuries. Claims that Jesus had once cured Veronica of a blood illness remain unproven.

Left St Veronica's veil is clearly imprinted with the image of Jesus Christ (the Master of Saint Veronica, Germany, c.1420).

JOSEPH OF ARIMATHEA

A SECRET BUT WEALTHY CONVERT TO CHRISTIANITY RESCUED THE
BODY OF CHRIST AFTER THE CRUCIFIXION. HE LAID IT TO REST IN
THE TOMB HE HAD PREPARED FOR HIMSELF.

KEY FACTS
*Cared for the dead body
of Jesus*
DATES: *1st century AD*
BIRTH PLACE: *Jerusalem*
PATRON OF: *Grave diggers,
burial, cemetery keepers and
caretakers*
FEAST DAY: *17 March*

Joseph was a wealthy Israelite who had secretly converted to Christianity. He did not take part in the Jewish condemnation of Jesus, nor did he speak against it.

Following the arrest of Jesus, the situation in Jerusalem was tense. Jewish leaders were calling for the punishment of this person who claimed to be the Messiah. But Pontius Pilate, the Roman governor, was reluctant to sentence Jesus to death.

To mark the Jewish festival of Passover, Pilate offered to pardon one prisoner, giving the Jews a

*Below Joseph of Arimathea preaches
to the inhabitants of Britain (William
Blake, 18th century).*

choice between Jesus and the common thief, Barabbas. Pilate was shocked by their choice and washed his hands to indicate his innocence. "Let his blood be upon us," the irate crowd replied. No doubt many Christians, like Joseph of Arimathea, did not dare face the mob.

THE TOMB OF CHRIST

Overwhelmed by shame at his cowardice after the Crucifixion, Joseph went to Pontius Pilate and asked for the body of Jesus. It was the custom to throw the bodies of criminals as carrion for animals to devour. But Joseph bought the mutilated body before this happened, and took it to a garden he

owned, close to Calvary where Jesus had died. Here, Joseph had carved out a rocky sepulchre intended as his own burial place. He wrapped the body in clean linen, pushing a huge rock against the opening to close the tomb.

LEGENDARY TRAVELS

It is said that the apostle Philip sent Joseph on a mission to England where he founded a church at Glastonbury and grew a tree that is said to flower on Christmas Day. Joseph is included in the Arthurian legends.

MARY MAGDALENE

LOVED FOR HER DEVOTION TO JESUS, MARY MAGDALENE IS THE GRAND EXAMPLE OF THE REFORMED SINNER. HER LIFE SHOWS THAT ANYONE MAY BE TRANSFORMED IF THEY TRULY REPENT.

KEY FACTS
First witness to the risen Christ
DATES: *1st century AD*
BIRTH PLACE: *Possibly Magdala, Palestine*
PATRON OF: *Repentant sinners, hairdressers, perfume-makers, contemplatives*
FEAST DAY: *22 July*
EMBLEM: *Jar of ointment, loosened hair*

Mary Magdalene was one of the many women who accompanied Jesus and the apostles on their travels, caring for them and supporting them. She was close to Jesus and played a major role in the events surrounding his death and resurrection.

CONTROVERSIAL FIGURE
Over the centuries Mary Magdalene has aroused much controversy among theologians.

In Western Christianity, she is often identified both as the sister of Martha of Bethany and as the sinner who dried Christ's feet with her hair. But in Eastern Christianity, Mary Magdalene, Martha of Bethany and the sinner are three different women.

Despite these problems, the existence of Mary Magdalene is not questioned. She is known for her sincere conversion, generous heart and contemplative mind.

Above Detail of Mary kissing Jesus' feet from Life of Saint Mary Magdalene *(attr. to Giotto di Bondone, Palmerino di Guido and others, 14th century).*

REPENTANT SINNER
The story of the sinner is perhaps the most significant of the earlier accounts thought to relate to Mary Magdalene.

While Jesus was dining at the home of a Pharisee called Simon, a woman crept in and knelt before him. Simon was angered by this interruption from a woman who was a known sinner.

The woman began to kiss Jesus' feet and weep, begging to be forgiven for her transgressions. She dried his feet with her long hair and rubbed them with

Left Mary Magdalene Reading *(attr. to Ambrosius Benson, 1540).*

Above Christ on the Cross with Saints *(Luca Signorelli and Pietro Perugino, 1482).*

expensive perfumed ointment. Jesus told the distraught woman that all her sins were forgiven.

MESSENGER OF CHRIST

To modern Christians, both Orthodox and Catholic, Mary Magdalene is important because she was a devoted and committed follower of Christ who witnessed some of the most significant moments of his life. She accom-

panied Jesus on his last journey to Jerusalem and was present at the Crucifixion, keeping vigil.

Three days after his death, Mary went to his burial cave, intending to anoint his body. When she arrived she found the rock that closed the cave opening had been rolled away and the body was gone. Mary ran to question a gardener nearby. But when he spoke she realized that he was the risen Christ. Jesus gave her the glory of telling the disciples that he had been resurrected.

PREACHER AND HERMIT

Eastern legend claims that, after the Resurrection, Mary Magdalene travelled to Ephesus with the Blessed Virgin and the apostle

> "Saint Mary Magdalene, teach us to forgive ourselves, and then to forgive others"
>
> PRAYER TO ST MARY MAGDALENE

Above Mary Magdalene carried by angels (Simon Vouet, 17th century).

John, where she later died and was buried. According to a Western legend, however, Mary, along with her sister Martha and brother Lazarus, travelled by boat to France. They landed in Provence and proceeded to Marseilles, where they preached the Gospel. Mary is said to have retired to a nearby cave to live as a hermit. When she died, angels carried her to the oratory of St Maximus near Aix-en-Provence.

MARTHA

Martha was either the sister of Mary of Bethany or, as in the Western Christian tradition, the sister of Mary Magdalene. Jesus was said to enjoy visiting Martha's house and loved her and her siblings. It was Martha's brother, Lazarus, whom Jesus raised from the dead.

A popular story reveals Martha's busy nature. On one of Jesus' visits to their home, she bustled about preparing food, while Mary sat in rapt attention at the feet of Christ. When Martha expressed irritation at her sister's idleness, Jesus rebuked her. He told her that Mary had made the better choice; the contemplative life is preferable to an active one that allows no time for thought or prayer.

Above The Raising of Lazarus *(the Coetivy Master, c.1460). Martha was chief among the mourners to witness the miracle.*

JAMES THE GREAT

ABANDONING HIS FISHING NETS IN ORDER TO BECOME A "FISHER OF MEN", JAMES WAS ONE OF THE EARLIEST DISCIPLES TO FOLLOW JESUS, AND THE FIRST APOSTLE MARTYR.

KEY FACTS
Apostle
DATES: *d.AD 44*
BIRTH PLACE: *Galilee*
PATRON OF: *Spain, Guatemala, Nicaragua; and, with Philip, of Uruguay*
FEAST DAY: *25 July*
EMBLEM: *Shell, sword, pilgrim's staff, pilgrim's hat*

There were two apostles named James. One became known as James the Less and the other, James the Great – so-called because he was the elder of the two. James the Great was one of the leading apostles.

James and his brother John were fishermen who abandoned their nets to follow Jesus. Both brothers were known to be quick-tempered, hence their nickname "sons of thunder".

James also had qualities of reliability, leadership and loyalty. He witnessed the major events of Christ's life. He was one of those present at the Transfiguration, and was in the garden of Gethsemane to comfort his master during his most despairing moments.

The details of James' life after the Crucifixion are uncertain. He may have gone to Judea and Samaria to spread the Christian

Above The shell and pilgrim's staff identify St James the Great (Hans Klocker, c. 17th century).

Below Apostles Philip and James are often portrayed as men of learning (School of Fra Bartolommeo, c. 1400).

message. But it is known that he was beheaded by Herod Agrippa in Jerusalem.

His body, it is said, was carried to the shore where a boat suddenly materialized. His disciples placed the body in this miraculous vessel and it floated to the coast of Spain. There, Christians found the relics and buried them in a forest where the city of Santiago de Compostela now stands.

The shrine containing his relics in Compostela was of great importance during the Crusades, because soldiers believed St James could grant military prowess. Santiago de Compostela remains a major site of modern pilgrimage.

GROWTH OF HIS CULTUS

According to Spanish tradition James appeared to fight the Moors when they invaded Spain in AD 844. He rode through the sky on a white horse, holding a shield bearing a red cross and a sword. With his help, the Spanish vanquished their enemy.

In the 16th century, sailors allegedly saw St James resting on a cloud. It hovered protectively over the galleons carrying early Spanish explorers across the Atlantic to the Americas. He inspired them to convert the American people they encountered. The feast day of St James the Great is celebrated in major national festivals in South America to this day.

JAMES THE LESS

THIS APOSTLE IS IDENTIFIED AS "THE SON OF ALPHAEUS" BUT HE SLIPS QUIETLY, ALMOST ANONYMOUSLY, THROUGH THE CHRISTIAN STORY. SOME SOURCES IDENTIFY HIM AS CHRIST'S BROTHER.

KEY FACTS
Apostle
DATES: *d. AD 62*
BIRTH PLACE: *Galilee*
PATRON OF: *The dying*
FEAST DAY: *3 May*
EMBLEM: *Fuller's club*

There is little mention of James the Less during Jesus' ministry. But after the Crucifixion and Resurrection, this James communicated closely with Jesus before his Ascension into heaven.

James became an important figure in the new Christian community in Jerusalem where St Paul relied on his leadership. During the Council of Jerusalem (*c.*AD 50), James supported Paul in the call to accept Gentiles as Christians without demanding these converts be circumcized. This decision caused much controversy at the council. As men brought up in the Jewish tradition, the apostles tended to regard circumcision as an important symbol of faith.

James was stoned or possibly clubbed to death. Another version says James was thrown from a temple top, but as he lay dying, he forgave his tormentors. Even Jewish leaders of the time believed the city faced calamity after the death of this fine man. James is often linked with the apostle Philip, and many churches are dedicated to "Philip and James".

Right The Communion of the Apostle James the Less *(Niccoló Bambini, 1720).*

PHILIP

THIS PRACTICAL-MINDED APOSTLE HELPED IN THE FEEDING OF THE 5,000, AND THE SEARCHING QUESTIONS HE ASKED JESUS CLARIFIED IMPORTANT POINTS OF FAITH.

KEY FACTS
Apostle
DATES: *1st century AD*
BIRTH PLACE: *Bethsaida*
PATRON OF: *Uruguay*
FEAST DAY: *3 May (West)*
EMBLEM: *Loaf of bread, large cross, a dragon*

Philip heard John the Baptist preach and then sought out Jesus. Philip seems to have been an energetic and practical man. He arranged appointments, and introduced Nathanael, later St Bartholomew, to Christ.

When Jesus wanted to feed a crowd of 5,000 people who had gathered to hear his message, Philip commented, "Two hundred pennyworth of bread is not sufficient for them". But when a small boy offered five loaves and two fishes, Philip helped distribute the food, believing this would feed everyone as Jesus said.

Above The Apostle Philip *(Georges de La Tour, 1620).*

At the Last Supper, Philip asked, "Lord, show us the Father". The answer came from Jesus, "I am in the Father and the Father is in me."

Philip preached in Phrygia and is thought to have killed an evil dragon brought by the Scythians. He possibly died a martyr in Hierapolis (in Syria), but his relics are held in Rome. He is closely associated with James the Less. The two apostles share a feast day.

PETER

CHRIST DESCRIBED PETER AS THE "ROCK OF THE CHURCH". AS THE
LEADER OF THE APOSTLES, HE IS THE EARTHLY FATHER OF THE FAITH,
AND IS SAID TO HOLD THE KEYS TO THE KINGDOM OF HEAVEN.

KEY FACTS
*Leader of the apostles; called the
rock of the Church by Jesus*
DATES: *d.c.AD 64*
BIRTH PLACE: *Bethsaida,
Sea of Galilee*
PATRON OF: *Fishermen, papacy*
FEAST DAY: *29 June*
EMBLEM: *Keys, ship, fish, cockerel*

Peter was warm and impetuous by nature, yet also rather cautious. He needed reassurance that Jesus was indeed the Messiah.

To his eternal shame, he was so overwhelmed by fear during the trial of Jesus that three times he denied his friendship with him. But Peter's passion and general boldness made him leader of the apostles. His name, Cephas in Aramaic, means "rock" and Jesus chose him as the "rock" upon which the Church was built.

Known as Simon Peter, he fished with his brother Andrew on the Sea of Galilee. Jesus came to them one day when they had failed to catch any fish. He told them to lower their nets and to their surprise they hauled up an enormous catch. "Come with

Above A mural showing Peter's denial of Christ and the cock crowing (from the Church of the Holy Cross at Platanistasa, Cyprus, 15th century).

me," Jesus said, "and I will make you fishers of men." After this, Peter began his ministry with Jesus, and he is mentioned frequently throughout the gospels. He was very close to Christ and became the leader of the 12 apostles. He was with Jesus during the Agony in the Garden, the night

Christ spent in tormented prayer before his arrest and death. And when the soldiers came that dawn to make the arrest, Peter was so enraged that he sliced off the ear of Judas Iscariot, the man who had betrayed Jesus to the authorities to his eternal shame.

Peter was one of three apostles to witness the Transfiguration when Jesus was surrounded by light with the prophets, Moses and Elijah, on either side. A voice said, "This is my beloved Son… Listen to Him." And after Pentecost, when the Holy Spirit gave the apostles the gift of tongues, Peter was the first to speak to the crowds.

FIRST CHURCH LEADER

Peter took administrative control of the apostles after Christ's death and chose Matthias to replace Judas Iscariot. He sent Paul and Barnabas to the Mediterranean as disciples and evangelists.

Peter cured a beggar who had suffered all his life from a lame leg, thus becoming the first apostle to perform a miracle. More significantly, he was ready to sit at a meal with a non-Jew, or Gentile. Peter converted a Roman centurion, Cornelius, who was the first Gentile to become a Christian believer.

The admittance of Gentiles caused controversy among the other apostles who had preached

Below Peter enthroned and six scenes from the lives of Jesus and St Peter (the Master of St Peter, 1280).

only to other Jews. They regarded the diet of non-Jews as unclean. But Peter had the support of Paul, who, like him, was determined to spread Christianity to everyone. Peter's frequent public preaching led to his arrest by Herod, who imprisoned him under heavy guard. But the apostle escaped, helped – it was said – by an angel who broke his chains and opened the prison doors.

This convinced Peter that he had truly been chosen to lead. He wrote letters and preached unceasingly, while organizing from Jerusalem the appointment and missions of evangelists.

Some authorities credit Peter with introducing the concept of "episcopal succession". In finding a replacement for Judas Iscariot, he began a system of choosing leaders from men who were familiar with the first apostles. This gave rise to the tradition that bishops and priests had a special closeness to Christ, and ensured that the status of priests remained separate from their flock.

When Peter visited Rome, he was arrested for his Christian activities and tried by the

Below Peter is dressed in papal splendour as he observes the Crucifixion (Ottaviano di Martino Nelli, 1424).

CORNELIUS

Cornelius (not to be confused with the Gentile Roman centurion) was an heir to Peter who became "bishop" of Rome in 251. He followed Peter in teaching that the Church must be conciliatory in its embrace. He favoured a lenient approach towards Christians who had lapsed. Another priest, Novatian, thought those who committed adultery, murder or even made a second marriage, should be expelled from the Church. Cornelius asserted that the Church had the power to forgive and welcome the repentant back to the community. The inscription "Cornelius martyr" inscribed on his tomb can be seen in the crypt of Lucina, in Rome.

Right This reliquary of St Cornelius, dating from 1350–60, is made of gold and silver.

"You are Peter
and upon this rock
I will build my church."

JESUS SPEAKING
TO PETER

Emperor Nero, who condemned him to death by crucifixion. Legend has it that Peter asked to be hung upside down on the cross because he was not worthy of dying in the same way as Christ.

Some claim that he died on the same day as Paul, and they share a feast day. For two centuries after

Peter's death, letters which were supposedly written by him were distributed in order to revive his lessons and maintain his influence.

He was buried in a tomb beneath the Vatican. Believers consider him the keeper of the gates to heaven, the saint who can let them enter the kingdom, or deny them entry when they die. Peter's enduring popularity is shown by the dedication of 1,129 churches to him in England alone.

Below Peter was the first apostle to perform a miracle. In this painting St John and St Peter heal a lame man (Masolino da Panicale, 1425).

MATTHEW

THE PRESUMED AUTHOR OF THE
FIRST GOSPEL WAS A FORMER
TAX COLLECTOR.

There are few stories about Matthew, also known as Levi. Little is known too about his life as an evangelist. He is presumed to be the author of the first gospel, written in an easy style for public reading.

Matthew was a tax collector, one of the hated class of Jews who collected money on behalf of the Roman authorities. His fellow Jews not only regarded this close contact with Gentiles as unclean, but also distrusted tax-men and believed they were corrupt. When Jesus approached Matthew, and

Above Saint Matthew *from* The Book of Kells, *an illuminated manuscript,* c.*AD 800.*

was even prepared to eat with him, he immediately rose from his counting table and followed him.

After Christ's Ascension to heaven, Matthew became a missionary like the other apostles but his journeys are not recorded.

An apocryphal story says that Matthew was martyred in Ethiopia defending an abbess. His reputed relics were transported to Salerno in Italy via Brittany. Others say he died in Persia.

JOHN

THE DISCIPLE WHOM JESUS LOVED AND ENTRUSTED HIS MOTHER TO
AFTER HIS DEATH IS THOUGHT TO BE THE AUTHOR OF THE FOURTH
GOSPEL, THREE EPISTLES AND THE BOOK OF REVELATION.

John and James the Great were two fiery-tempered brothers, sons of Zebedee. Both were called from mending their fishing nets to follow Jesus.

John's ardour could turn him to brave and reckless endeavours. However, Jesus' faith in John was apparent at the Crucifixion. When he was facing death, Jesus put his mother, Mary, the Blessed Virgin, into John's care rather than choose anyone else.

The belief that he was a favourite disciple is confirmed by the facts of John's life. He was with Jesus at the Miracle of the Loaves and Fishes. With Peter and James, he witnessed the Transfiguration, and he was by the side of Jesus during the Agony in the Garden of Gethsemane.

John was placed at the right hand of Christ at the Last Supper, and he was the only disciple not to desert Jesus during the horrors

Left This woodcarving depicts John's anguish and horror during Christ's crucifixion at Calvary (Ferdinand Maximilian Brokof, 18th century).

of the Crucifixion. He kept vigil at the foot of the Cross, and then showed no hesitation in accepting Jesus had risen from the dead.

After the Ascension, John worked with St Peter organizing the early Christian Church. After some years, he was exiled to Patmos, a Greek island. One of the greatest Christian evangelists, it is thought he died at a great age in Ephesus, Turkey.

MARK

THE AUTHOR OF THE SECOND
GOSPEL INTERPRETED AND
RECORDED PETER'S TEACHING.

M ark was young when he first met Jesus. His mother's house was a favourite meeting place for the apostles and Jesus often visited.

Although Mark was not an apostle, he seems to have been charming and affectionate, though not brave or confident. It was rumoured that he ran away from the Roman soldiers who arrested Jesus. And he abandoned a difficult mission with St Peter to Cyprus. But when older, he gave St Paul much support during his arrest in Rome. St Peter even referred to him fondly as his son.

Mark travelled widely as an evangelist, visiting Jerusalem, Rome and Egypt. He may have travelled to Alexandria and become the first bishop of that city. Mark's gospel incorporates many of Peter's teachings and memoirs, so it is likely it was written in Rome where the two men spent long periods together.

Despite Mark's important role in the Christian story as the writer of the Second Gospel, his place and manner of death are uncertain. He is thought to have died sometime after Jerusalem was destroyed in AD 70. A legend claims he was tied round the neck and dragged through the streets of Alexandria. His bodily relics were carried by the Venetians to Venice where they were placed in the basilica named after him, St Mark's Basilica.

Right St Mark's famous emblem, the winged lion, sits at his feet (the Ulm Master, 1442).

The relics survived a fire in the church in AD 976, and were installed in the new building. A series of mosaics in the church tell the story of St Mark and the translation of his relics.

Left A statue of St Mark by the early Renaissance sculptor Donatello (1411–15). St Mark's image appears widely in Italy.

His emblem is a winged lion. This refers to the inspiration Mark derived from John the Baptist, who lived in the wilderness with animals. Mark became the patron saint of Venice. His lion emblem can be found on the façades of many buildings across the Greek Ionian islands, where medieval Venice held dominion.

LUKE

THE PHYSICIAN AND WRITER OF THE THIRD GOSPEL WAS A MOST SYMPATHETIC MAN WHO, UNUSUALLY FOR THE TIME, INCLUDED IN HIS WORK THE WOMEN WHO WERE IMPORTANT IN THE LIFE OF JESUS.

St Luke was a Greek doctor. His writings contain observations of women and human suffering, and reveal him to be gentle and sensitive. St Paul probably converted Luke, a Gentile of Antioch, and persuaded him to travel with him on evangelical voyages around the Mediterranean.

More than any other New Testament writer, Luke shows us the women in Jesus' life. Thanks to him, we know more about Mary Magdalene and about the widow whose son Jesus restored to life.

Luke tells the story of Mary and the Annunciation, and also mentions Elizabeth, mother of John the Baptist. He is deeply respectful of the Virgin Mary and apparently knew her. The words

Above This enamel plaque showing St Luke was made in the workshop of the Kremlin (17th century).

Below St Luke Drawing the Virgin (Rogier van der Weyden, 15th century). Luke was a talented painter as well as writer.

KEY FACTS
Writer of the Third Gospel
DATES: *1st century AD*
BIRTH PLACE: *Antioch, Syria*
PATRON OF: *Surgeons, doctors, painters and glass artists*
FEAST DAY: *18 October*
EMBLEM: *Winged ox*

he puts into her mouth when he describes the Annunciation are known as "Mary's Prayer", and have become part of the liturgy.

A HUMANE APPROACH

Luke emphasizes gentle aspects of the faith. He repeats the most moving parables that Jesus told to show examples of goodness and kindness. However, his gospel does open with the story of the bull sacrificed by Zachary to celebrate the birth of his son, John the Baptist. This accounts for Luke's emblem, a winged ox.

He also wrote *The Acts of the Apostles*, a mixture of history and prophecy describing the spread of Christianity. He explains how the faith broke with Judaism, and extended beyond Jerusalem to Rome in the West.

Luke also has a reputation as a painter. There are many portraits of the Virgin attributed to St Luke in the Christian world, though unfortunately none are authenticated. The church of St Augustine in Rome has several such portraits. It is said Luke lived to a great age and never married.

"My soul doth magnify the Lord,
And my spirit hath rejoiced in God my Saviour"

LUKE 1:46

STEPHEN

THE FIRST CHRISTIAN MARTYR WAS CRUELLY STONED TO DEATH IN JERUSALEM FOR HIS BELIEFS.

The first ever Christian martyr was a learned Jew and one of the first deacons. After his conversion, Stephen took control of almsgiving to elderly widows in his community. When he began to preach he often criticized some aspects of Jewish Mosaic law.

After Stephen had made some particularly hostile allegations, his Jewish listeners became outraged. He accused them of resisting the true Spirit and being responsible for the death of Christ.

KEY FACTS
First martyr
DATES: *d.c.AD 35*
BIRTH PLACE: *Jerusalem*
PATRON OF: *Bricklayers, stonemasons, builders, deacons*
FEAST DAY: *26 December (West)*
EMBLEM: *Stones, the palm of martyrdom, a book*

The mob stoned him to death with the consent of a man called Saul, a Roman Jew. Saul later converted and became Paul, the great Christian leader.

Left The stoning of St Stephen as depicted in a stained glass window (St Edmundsbury Cathedral, Suffolk, England, 19th century).

EUSTACE

THE HERO OF THIS LEGEND CHASES A STAG THAT BEARS THE CROSS OF CHRIST WITHIN ITS ANTLERS. THIS EXPERIENCE LEADS TO HIS CONVERSION AND HIS UNTIMELY DEATH.

Fabulous stories surround the figure of St Eustace. Named Placidas at birth, he became a high-ranking Roman soldier and was a keen huntsman.

One day he stalked a stag deep in the forest. As he lifted his bow, the stag turned. A gleaming crucifix grew between its antlers. Then the stag said, "I am Jesus, whom you honour without knowing".

Placidas, his wife and children converted to Christianity and he was baptized as Eustace. They suffered many misfortunes and Eustace's faith was tested to the limits. His wife was seduced (or raped) and his children sold into slavery. Later, their luck changed for the better when Eustace was

KEY FACTS
Miracle appearance of the crucifix
DATES: *Unknown*
BIRTH PLACE: *Unknown*
PATRON OF: *Hunters and those in difficult situations*
FEAST DAY: *2 November (West; officially de-canonized)*
EMBLEM: *Stag bearing a crucifix*

reunited with his family in Rome. He was honoured for a military victory, but unfortunately this good luck did not last, and when he refused to make a pagan sacrifice, he and his family were thrown to the lions in the arena. The beasts refused to attack, so the entire family was burnt inside a brazen bull – a form of execution devised by the ancient Greeks, akin to being boiled alive.

Left The Vision of Saint Eustace (Albrecht Dürer, 16th century).

POLYCARP

A TRUE SHEPHERD TO HIS FLOCK, THE BISHOP OF SMYRNA WAS ONE OF THE APOSTOLIC FATHERS OF THE CHURCH. HE GUIDED IT THROUGH DANGERS OF HERESY AND INTERNAL DISPUTES IN ROME.

KEY FACTS
Apostolic Father of the Church
DATES: c.*AD 69–155*
BIRTH PLACE: *Possibly Syria*
FEAST DAY: *23 February*

Polycarp knew the apostles, particularly St John. He was the living link between those who had known Christ in the flesh and the next generation of believers. This made him an Apostolic Father, and with this authority he played a significant role in the early Church.

During a wave of paganism in Asia in the 2nd century AD, Polycarp kept an strong hold on the essentials of Christ's teaching. He fought heretical or radical interpretations and practices, and his firm stand strengthened the spread of the Church in the East.

A heretical sect leader who wished to have a debate with Polycarp was rebuffed with the phrase, "I recognize you as the first-born of Satan". In his own writing, Polycarp explained, "For every one who shall not confess that Jesus Christ has come in the flesh is the antichrist".

St Irenaeus of Lyons was a child when he first heard Polycarp preach and recount his memories of the apostles. Irenaeus has left letters mentioning Polycarp, who was the bishop of Smyrna for almost 50 years. These letters give

Left Saint Sebastian and Saint Polycarp Destroying the Idols *(Pedro Garcia de Benabarre, 15th century). Broken idols litter the floor.*

glimpses of his life and his high standing in the Church. Ignatius of Antioch, awaiting martyrdom in Rome, trusted Polycarp to receive and forward secret letters on his behalf.

In old age, Polycarp was called to Rome to discuss the timing of feast days, especially that of Easter. He met Anicetus, bishop of Rome. They agreed to disagree, and Polycarp returned to Smyrna, believing his community could now peacefully use the calendar that it preferred.

MARTYRDOM

He was over 80 when a mob bayed for his blood. Excited by pagan festivities that included lions attacking Christians, they shouted, "This is the father of the Christians". The Roman consul refused to throw Polycarp into the arena, but conceded to a death by burning. At the stake, Polycarp said, "May I be received among the martyrs in your presence today as a rich and pleasing sacrifice." A soldier stabbed him in order to spare him the pain of burning. Christians gathered relics from the ashes, and wrote an account of the trial and death of this martyr-saint, giving evidence of an early cultus.

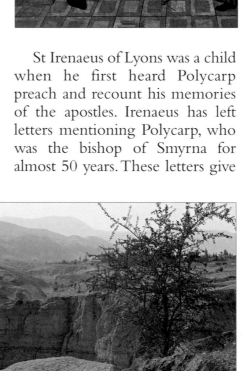

Left St Polycarp spread the Christian faith in the sometimes rugged terrain of Palestine (left) and Syria.

JUSTIN

THIS CHRISTIAN PHILOSOPHER
EXPLAINED THE MESSAGE OF
CHRIST IN HIS WRITINGS.

Justin was well educated and
sought answers to life's problems through philosophy. But the
teachings of Pythagorus, Plato
and the Stoics brought him no
closer to the Almighty.

CONVERSION

A chance encounter with a
stranger directed him to look for
meaning in the message of
Christ. When Justin converted to
the faith he was about 30 years
old. The Christians he met were
reluctant to discuss their rituals
with an outsider. Justin said, "It is
our duty to make known our
doctrine, lest we incur the guilt
and the punishment of those who
have sinned through ignorance."

Justin wrote the *Apologies* and
Dialogues, important fragments of
which have survived. In these
writings, he sets out the moral
values of the faith and presents a
philosophical proof of its truth.

He is recognized as the first
Christian apologist. Dressed as a
philosopher, he preached and
taught throughout Palestine, Syria
and other regions.

TRIAL AND DEATH

In Rome, he had a public debate
with another philosopher, named
Crescens. Justin presented the
more convincing argument, and
his adversary is believed to have
later instigated his arrest. A record
of his trial survives. The martyr
confessed his faith unhesitatingly,
and gave courage to six other
Christians who were also on trial.
Justin was decapitated, in accordance with Roman law.

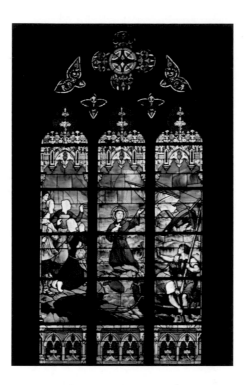

KEY FACTS
Apologist (vindicator) of the faith
DATES: c.*AD 100–65*
BIRTH PLACE: *Flavia Neapolis*
(now Nablus, Palestine)
PATRON OF: *Philosophers*
FEAST DAY: *1 June*
EMBLEM: *Philosopher's clothes*

Left A stained-glass window depicting
St Justin preaching to fishermen in
stormy weather.

Below A Sailor Offering a
Model Boat to St Justin (*Domenico
Robusti Tintoretto, son of Jacopo,
c. 17th century*).

IRENAEUS OF LYONS

THE BISHOP OF LYONS WAS AN INFLUENTIAL THEOLOGIAN WHO HELPED THE CHURCH TO CLARIFY THE ARTICLES OF CHRISTIAN FAITH, IN PARTICULAR THE UNITY OF THE FATHER AND THE SON.

KEY FACTS
Venerated as a martyr
DATES: *c.AD 130–200*
BIRTH PLACE: *Possibly Smyrna*
FEAST DAY: *28 June (West)*
EMBLEM: *Bishop's clothes*

As a theologian St Irenaeus was not only able to defend and explain Christianity theoretically, he could also preach it to laymen.

Irenaeus worked as a priest in Lyons. He was sent to Rome on a peacemaking mission by his bishop Pothinus in AD 177. He took a message to the pope to show leniency towards the North African Church whose practices differed from those of Rome. He also brokered a compromise between the East and Pope Victor III who wanted Rome to decree the dates for Easter.

On his return, Irenaeus became Bishop of Lyons as his predecessor had been killed. Under his care the faith spread through this rich merchant city. He was the first to make a systematic organization of Catholic beliefs. His writings distinguished faith from the then popular heresy, Gnosticism, and he enhanced the unity of the faithful.

He wrote the "rule of faith" that encompasses all "the riches of Christian truth", still delivered at baptisms. He died at Lyons, but unfortunately his shrine was destroyed in the Reformation.

Above St Irenaeus resurrects and baptizes a girl in this Belgian tapestry.

COSMAS AND DAMIAN

THE TWIN DOCTORS WHO NEVER CHARGED FOR THE MEDICAL CARE THEY GAVE HAVE LONG BEEN VENERATED FOR THEIR HEALING SKILLS AND THEIR KINDNESS. AS SUCH, THEY ARE PATRONS OF DOCTORS.

KEY FACTS
Doctors, miracle cures
DATES: *Unknown*
BIRTH PLACE: *Syria*
PATRON OF: *Doctors, dentists, barbers, chemists, hairdressers*
FEAST DAY: *26 September (West)*
EMBLEM: *Ampoules and medicine jars*

A widespread cultus followed Sts Cosmas and Damian in the 5th century AD. They practised as doctors in Cyrrhus, Syria, where a famous basilica was erected.

With wonderful powers of healing, aided by the Holy Spirit, they were known as the "holy moneyless ones" because their medical care was free. They also looked after sick animals.

Although Cosmas and Damian were persecuted by the Romans, it was said that rocks thrown at the twins simply flew backwards. Neither did the torture rack function. A further account says that after their eventual deaths by

beheading, the twins returned to earth to save Justinianus, deacon of their church. He lost a leg and they replaced the pale limb with another one from a black-skinned Ethiopian man. Differing versions of this story have been depicted by artists over the years.

Sick believers took to sleeping in the twins' church, hoping this "incubation" would cure them – a practice known also to occur in other religions.

Right Healing of the Deacon Justinianus by the Saints Cosmas and Damian (*Fra Angelico, 1440*). *The new black leg is clearly visible.*

PERPETUA

A YOUNG MOTHER RECORDED HER EXPERIENCES AND VISIONS WHILE AWAITING MARTYRDOM.

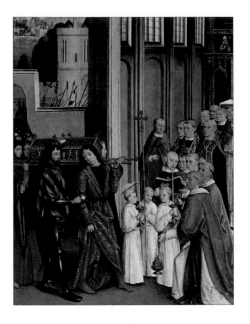

Above The shrine of St Perpetua is transferred to the Church of Bouvignes after the Siege of Dinant in 1466 (Flemish School, 15th century).

KEY FACTS
Martyr
DATES: *d.AD 203*
BIRTH PLACE: *Carthage*
FEAST DAY: *7 March*

The daughter of a wealthy pagan in Carthage, Perpetua was arrested during a Roman persecution of newly converted Christians. Perpetua was first placed under house arrest, then imprisoned, even though she was the mother of a young baby.

She was 22 years old when she wrote about her extraordinary experiences. The work, finished anonymously, is an authentic record of Christian martyrdom.

She mentions her worries about her father and baby and describes vivid dreams of ladders to heaven and her dead brother, but the most inspiring vision was one of herself, changed into a man, fighting the devil.

Perpetua was allowed to send her baby home before her death. Some say she entered the arena at Carthage singing joyfully. She was wounded by a mad heifer, then despatched by the sword.

FELICITAS

ST PERPETUA'S HANDMAIDEN RISKED HER OWN LIFE AND THAT OF HER UNBORN CHILD WHEN SHE ACCEPTED THE CHRISTIAN FAITH. SHE WAS MARTYRED AT THE SAME TIME AS HER MISTRESS.

KEY FACTS
Martyr
DATES: *d.AD 203*
BIRTH PLACE: *Carthage*
FEAST DAY: *7 March*

This young woman was a slave of St Perpetua in the Roman colony of Carthage. When her mistress was arrested, Felicitas (or Felicity) went with her to prison.

Felicitas was heavily pregnant at the time of their detention. Her husband, Revocatus, and two other slaves, Saturninus and Secundulus, were also caught up in the persecution. While under house arrest, they were all baptized before their transfer to prison.

Incarcerated in a filthy cell, Felicitas went into a difficult labour and brutal warders jeered at her pain. She knew her fate and that of her husband was death in the arena, so was grateful to give birth beforehand. A free Christian adopted the baby girl.

Above The ancient Punic city walls of Carthage in present-day Tunisia. For the saints' martyrdom in the city's arena, leopards and bears were prepared to attack the men, and a mad heifer directed toward the two women.

DENYS OF PARIS

CREDITED WITH THE FOUNDING OF THE CHRISTIAN CHURCH IN PARIS, THIS VIRTUOUS MAN WENT ON TO BECOME A BISHOP AND WAS LATER MARTYRED FOR HIS FAITH.

KEY FACTS
Early mission to France
DATES: *d.c.AD 250*
BIRTH PLACE: *Italy*
PATRON OF: *Paris and France, headaches*
FEAST DAY: *9 October*
EMBLEM: *Head held in his hands*

Said to be a fearless preacher, the Italian-born St Denys (or Dionysius) of Paris was sent on a dangerous mission to revive the persecuted Church of Gaul (France) in AD 250. Together with the deacon Eleutherius and the priest Rusticus, he established a Christian community on an island in the River Seine, close to Roman Paris.

St Denys' mission led to countless conversions, arousing the anger of the local pagan priests

Below The interior of the 12th-century monastery dedicated to St Denys, built on the site of his death in Paris. It is a fitting tribute to the patron saint of the city and France.

Above This baroque statue of St Denys is one in a group of the Fourteen Holy Helpers. Denys is shown carrying his severed head, still preaching, in accordance with the story.

who pushed for the missionaries to be stopped. The saint and his companions were eventually imprisoned and tortured before being beheaded on Montmartre (Martyrs' Hill) where the church of the Sacré Coeur now stands.

According to legend, a great miracle then occurred: St Denys picked up his head and walked two miles, preaching as he went. He eventually lay down and was buried with his fellow martyrs by a pious woman named Catulla.

Another version of events states that after they had been murdered the bodies of the martyrs were thrown into the Seine and retrieved and buried by converts. In both accounts, a shrine was built over the burial place, to be covered years later (*c.*AD 630) by a great abbey and church. This building, the Basilica of St-Denis later became the burial place of the kings of France.

A NATIONAL FIGURE

St Denys had become a figure of national devotion by the 9th century. This was partly due to a great medieval mix up. The Emperor Louis I of France had been given the writings of a certain Dionysius (or Pseudo Dionysius) in which the author claimed to know the apostles. To the people of the time this would have identified the author as Dionysius the Areopagite, who was converted to Christianity by St Paul.

When Louis commissioned Hilduin, Abbot of St-Denis, to write a biography of St Denys in 835, he asked the abbot to use the works of Pseudo Dionysius as his source. In Hilduin's book, Dionysius the Areopagite and St Denys became the same man. This fiction persisted for 700 years, until it was discovered that Pseudo Dionysius was in fact a 5th-century theologian and philosopher, and St Denys was a significant figure in his own right.

VALENTINE

TWO DIFFERENT VALENTINES WERE MARTYRS DURING THE ROMAN PERIOD, AND IT WAS ONLY DURING THE 14TH CENTURY THAT THE SAINT'S NAME BECAME ASSOCIATED WITH LOVERS.

There seem to be two saints with this name. One was a 2nd-century bishop of Terni, Italy, the other a 3rd-century priest in Rome; both were martyred. Some hagiographers claim they were one and the same person.

The 3rd-century Valentinus was reportedly imprisoned for helping Christians, then tried to convert the Emperor Claudius II, cured his jailer's daughter of blindness, and was beheaded outside Rome's Flaminian Gate.

No one is sure why Valentine is associated with lovers. It may follow Lupercalia, an old pagan festival, celebrated in mid-February. On the eve of the Lupercalia, all the young women's names would be put into a container, and each young man would draw out a name. He would then be paired with the woman he had chosen for the remainder of the festival.

Another theory associates the courtship with a line by the English medieval poet Chaucer, who observed that birds choose their mates on 14 February.

Right St Valentine (painted glass, Hungarian School, 19th century).

KEY FACTS
Representative of hidden love and courtship
DATES: *3rd century AD*
BIRTH PLACE: *Unknown*
PATRON OF: *Lovers, betrothed couples, greetings*
FEAST DAY: *14 February*
EMBLEM: *Heart, birds, roses*

VICTOR OF MARSEILLES

THIS CONVERT, A SOLDIER, WAS SEVERELY PUNISHED FOR HIS FAITH AND HAD A STRONG CULTUS IN THE MEDIEVAL ERA. HIS TOMB BECAME A POPULAR PILGRIM SHRINE.

KEY FACTS
Venerated as a martyr
DATES: *3rd century AD*
BIRTH PLACE: *Marseilles, France*
PATRON OF: *Millers, lightning, torture victims, cabinet-makers*
FEAST DAY: *21 July*
EMBLEM: *Windmill, millstone*

Archaeological evidence points to the burial of a total of three martyrs beneath the church of St Victor in Marseilles. Tunnels and caves show early habitation, probably of monks.

Victor may have been a Moor in the Roman army who was converted. His fellow soldiers, fearing for his life, begged him to return to traditional Roman beliefs, but he refused. Legend says he was betrayed by other militia.

He was thrown into prison but his profound faith converted the two military wardens charged with guarding him. These two

Below Victor of Marseilles is shown as a brave soldier of the faith destroying false idols (Hermen Rode, 1481).

men were executed, and legend describes the cruel treatment meted out to Victor. He was put on the rack, and burned. His foot was hacked off and then he was crushed and ground between two large millstones.

Many miracles were claimed in his name and he developed a wide cultus in the medieval era. His tomb became one of the most visited pilgrim centres in what was then Gaul, and St-Victor Church can still be visited today.

CECILIA

ANGELS AND HEAVENLY MUSIC HELPED CECILIA TO CONVERT HER HUSBAND AND OTHERS.

When she was a young woman, Cecilia's family refused to accept that she had taken a vow of virginity and forced her to marry a pagan. During the wedding, Cecilia sang silently to the Lord, "My heart remain unsullied, so that I may not be confounded". The bride vowed that her marriage would never be consummated.

Cecilia kept strong in her faith and told her husband, Valerian, that an angel was guarding her. She said God would be angry if Valerian touched her, but if he desisted, God would love him. Furthermore, if her husband were baptized, he would see this angel.

Valerian converted and angels appeared and placed flowers on the heads of the young couple. Cecilia's brother Tiburtius chose to become a Christian after this incident. In fact, the two men became so ardent in their faith that the Romans beheaded them, as Christianity was proscribed. Cecilia buried the two martyrs at her home. She, too, attracted anger

Above A terracotta statue of Cecilia in the cathedral in Le Mans, France (Charles Hoyay, 17th century).

from the state, but officials sent to arrest her were so overwhelmed by her faith that they converted.

Cecilia converted 400 people who were later baptized by Pope Urban in her home, which was later dedicated as a church.

The authorities did not abandon their persecution of Cecilia. They tried locking her in her own bathroom and burning the furnaces high. She lived through this ordeal, and then survived for three days after a soldier hacked at her neck with a sword.

There is little firm evidence for Cecilia's story. Her patronage of music comes from the heavenly sound she heard in her head while the organs played at her wedding.

ANASTASIA

Virgin martyrs such as Ursula and Cecilia have attracted legends of heroism and miracles. Other martyrs give their names to churches, or else linger in the religious folk memory.

One such figure is St Anastasia. Nothing is known about her. It is possible she was martyred at a place now known as Srem Mitrovica, Serbia. Her name is in the Roman Canon. A prayer is said to her at Mass, and a few antique Byzantine churches carry her name. She was a "matron", not a "maiden", so she is not counted as one of the virgin martyrs.

Below A stained-glass window depicting the martyrdom of St Anastasia (20th-century copy from a 13th-century original).

Left St Cecilia's tomb. Her body was found lying in this position in 1599, and the statue copies it exactly.

GEORGE

THE POTENCY OF HIS STORY ENSURES THAT ST GEORGE HOLDS A PLACE IN THE COMPANY OF SAINTS, BUT THE CHURCH SUSPECTS THAT THIS CHIVALROUS KNIGHT MAY BE MERELY A LEGEND.

In the 6th century, St George was described as good in so many ways that all his "deeds are known only to God". Sadly, most things about this saint remain known only by his maker, because evidence of his life is so sparse.

It seems certain, however, that George was a real martyr, a knight who came from Cappadocia in Turkey and died in Lydda (site of modern-day Lod) in Palestine.

GEORGE AND THE DRAGON
In what is undoubtedly his most famous legend, George was riding through Libya when he heard cries of mourning. Townspeople told him that they were being tyrannized by a dragon that they had to feed with two lambs a day. Now they had no lambs left and the dragon was demanding a human meal. They had drawn lots from the maidens and the king's daughter had been chosen. Dressed in a beautiful bridal gown, the princess had gone forth to meet her doom. St George dashed into action and crippled the monster by thrusting his lance into it. Tying her girdle round the dragon's neck, the princess led it limping to the town. The terrified citizens prepared to run, but George told them that if they would be baptized, the dragon would be slain. They all agreed. It was alleged that approximately 15,000 people were baptized. Four ox carts moved the beast's body to a distant meadow.

Right St George and the Dragon *(Paolo Uccello, c.1439–40).*

Above St George as depicted in a fresco in the Church of our Lady of the Pasture, Asinou, Cyprus (late 12th century).

CULTUSES AND CRUSADES
There are signs that St George's cultus was widespread early in Christian history. He was venerated across Europe and known in England before the Norman Conquest of AD 1066. His image can be found all over the Middle East, the Balkans and Greece.

During the Crusader battle of Antioch in AD 1098, Frankish (German) knights were blessed with a vision of George and another knight, St Demetrius. Possibly on his return from the Third Crusade a century later, Richard I promoted the veneration of St George in England.

PATRONAGE
St George is now the patron saint of England, as well as of boy scouts and soldiers, and many churches bear his name. In 1914, together with St John Chrysostom and St Roch, St George was declared a patron of Constantinople (Istanbul).

Because so little is actually known of St George, the Church downgraded him in 1960, and today his feast day is reduced to prayers during mass. But his name and his story of chivalry are loved across the world. His flag, a red cross on white background, was well known by the 14th century and is the national flag of England.

VITUS

A CHILD WHO DEFIED HIS PARENTS TO BECOME A CHRISTIAN, VITUS CURED SUFFERERS OF MENTAL ILLNESS AND EPILEPSY. FOLLOWERS DANCED ON HIS FEAST DAY TO ENSURE A YEAR OF GOOD HEALTH.

It is said that Vitus was a young boy when he elected to be baptized without his parents' knowledge. His angry parents beat him and threw him into a dungeon when he refused to give up his faith.

Above The façade of the neo-Gothic Cathedral of St Vitus in Prague.

Angels, dancing in a dazzling light, came to comfort him. His furious father visited him and tried to persuade Vitus to abandon the faith. But the angry man was blinded by the light and flitting movements of the dancing angels. He restored his father's sight, but this did not bring Vitus any peace.

As various other miracles were attributed to him, he found that officials became suspicious of him. Fearing for his safety, he fled from his birthplace in Sicily. He landed with two companions at Lucania in Italy where they stayed a while, preaching to the people. Finally they reached Rome, where Vitus cured Emperor Diocletian's son by expelling evil spirits that possessed the child.

KEY FACTS
Miracle worker
DATES: *d.c.AD 303*
BIRTH PLACE: *Sicily*
PATRON OF: *St Vitus' dance, actors, comedians, against lightning and storms, against epilepsy, protection against dangerous animals, Sicily*
FEAST DAY: *15 June*
EMBLEM: *Dog or cockerel*

But after this healing, Vitus was expected to make a thanksgiving sacrifice to the Roman gods who, it was presumed, had given him the power. Vitus refused, and so was branded a dangerous sorcerer.

Vitus and his companions were subjected to various unsuccessful tortures and were reputedly lifted to safety by an angel during a great storm. The site of their death or martyrdom remains unclear. Both St-Denis in Paris and Corvey in Saxony claim to hold his relics.

DYMPNA

A PRINCESS WHO FLED FROM HER OBSESSED FATHER BECAME PATRONESS OF THE INSANE.

Legend explains that Dympna was a princess, the daughter of a Celtic or heathen king. She grew up to be beautiful, but she also bore an uncanny resemblance to her dead mother.

Her father developed a perverted passion for his daughter, and so she fled with her confessor or teacher, St Gerebernus. The two fugitives made their way to Gheel, near Antwerp, in Belgium. They lived as hermits but the king

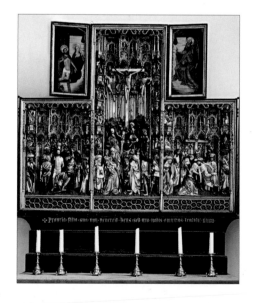

Above This intricate decorated altar is found in the St Dympna Church in Gheel, Belgium (c.1490–1500). It is called the Passion Altar, and it depicts the last days of Christ on earth.

KEY FACTS
Virgin, miracle worker
DATES: *c.7th century*
BIRTH PLACE: *Possibly Celtic Britain*
PATRON OF: *The mentally ill, against epilepsy and possession by the devil, sleepwalkers*
FEAST DAY: *30 May*

traced them and demanded her return. When the king's request was refused, he ordered his guards to murder Gerebernus and he beheaded his own daughter. Years later, the bones of the victims were discovered. After visiting these relics, numerous epileptics and lunatics claimed to be cured.

CHRISTOPHER

THE PATRON SAINT OF TRAVELLERS DERIVES HIS NAME FROM A GREEK WORD MEANING "ONE WHO CARRIES CHRIST". CHRISTOPHER IS LOVED FOR THIS HONOURABLE TASK.

KEY FACTS

Carried the child Jesus across a river
DATES: *Unknown*
BIRTH PLACE: *Unknown*
PATRON OF: *Wayfarers, travellers and motorists*
FEAST DAY: *25 July*
EMBLEM: *Pole to aid walking through the river, carrying a child on his shoulder*

One of the best-known saints, Christopher is now deemed legendary and no longer included in the Roman Calendar. However, this "de-canonization" has not stopped the popular veneration of St Christopher, whose image adorns cars and key rings. Travellers everywhere continue to pray for his intercession.

According to some stories, Christopher was a tall, muscular man. He is described in the *Golden Legend* as having a "fearful face and appearance".

Below This image from a German illuminated manuscript gives a realistic view of the agony St Christopher endured as he carried the small, but extraordinarily heavy infant Jesus across the river (15th century).

BECOMING A CHRISTIAN

Christopher found "a right great king" to serve, but soon observed he made the sign of the cross whenever hearing the word "devil". Christopher felt that needing such help was hardly fitting for a great monarch. So instead, he sought this powerful devil and worked for him.

With the devil leading him, Christopher travelled through the desert. The discovery that a cross, thrust into the sands, frightened the devil prompted Christopher to seek an explanation. A holy hermit told him about the power of this cross, and then converted him to Christianity.

Because of his size, Christopher dreaded fasting. Nor could he accept long hours of prayer and short periods of sleep. The hermit asked if Christopher could carry travellers across the river. In this way, the *Golden Legend* explains, he found a way to serve the Lord.

CARRYING CHRIST

A child once asked Christopher to carry him, so he hoisted the little boy on to his shoulders and stepped into the water. The child grew heavier, but Christopher persevered. On reaching the other bank, he felt "all the world upon me; I might bear no greater burden". The boy replied, "Thou hast not only borne all the world upon thee, but thou hast borne Him that made all the world, upon thy soldiers. I am Jesus Christ."

Christopher went to Lycia (southern Turkey) to preach but was arrested. He survived burning by iron rods, and when they shot him, the arrows stopped in mid-air. Finally they beheaded him.

The truth about Christopher is sparse. He was martyred in the Middle East, honoured in the 3rd century AD, and a church was dedicated to him in the 4th century AD. Early Christians prayed to his image to ensure safe travel, which has led to the practice today.

Below St Christopher is gaunt but noble in this sensitive wood carving (Gothic-style winged altar in the Kefermarkt, Austria, c.1490).

DOROTHY

FEARLESS IN THE FACE OF TORTURE AND DEFIANT IN DEATH, DOROTHY RETURNED TO WORK A MIRACLE, DELIVERING A GIFT FROM PARADISE TO A MAN WHO HAD TAUNTED HER FOR HER FAITH.

Despite coming from a noble Roman family in Caesarea in Cappadocia, Turkey, Dorothy would not pay homage to her family's pagan gods. Punished for her Christian faith and refusal to marry, she experienced frightful torture. But the weapons used against her felt as mere feathers.

At the place of execution, Dorothy showed no fear and instead announced to the crowd around her that she was glad to leave this cold world for one that knew neither ice nor snow. A young man called Theophilus, taunted her for both her virginity

KEY FACTS
Virgin martyr
DATES: *d.c.AD 304*
BIRTH PLACE: *Caesarea, Cappadocia*
PATRON OF: *Florists, gardeners, brewers and bridal couples*
FEAST DAY: *6 February*
EMBLEM: *Basket of flowers, especially roses, and of fruit*

and her faith. He then challenged her to send him roses and fruit when she reached her paradise.

In the winter after Dorothy's martyrdom, an angel delivered a basket filled with roses and fruit to Theophilus. He converted but the young man, too, was executed.

Left Theophilus taunts Dorothy in The Flower Miracle of Saint Dorothy *(Hans Baldung, 1516).*

VINCENT OF SARAGOSSA

SPAIN'S FIRST MARTYR SAINT WAS REVERED FOR HIS COURAGE AND STAMINA IN THE FACE OF REPEATED TORTURE. SYMBOLIC OF THIS RESISTANCE IS HIS SUPPOSED POWER AGAINST WINTER FROST.

There is little evidence about this early martyr saint, yet St Vincent of Saragossa was venerated across the Roman Empire. Every Christian community associated his name with Christ.

He is the protomartyr of Spain and his fate was horrible. Taken prisoner, Vincent was thrown into jail. He was kept on a starvation diet so that his body, and resolve, might weaken. Still he refused to recognize the pagan gods.

The authorities put him in the stocks, stretched him on the rack and roasted him on a gridiron. After that he was returned to his

KEY FACTS
Spain's first martyr
DATES: *d.AD 304*
BIRTH PLACE: *Saragossa, Spain*
PATRON OF: *Wine-growers, wine- and vinegar-makers, and of Portugal*
FEAST DAY: *22 January*
EMBLEM: *Dressed as a deacon holding a palm tree or on a gridiron*

miserable prison and left to starve. Vincent endured all this brutal violence with defiance and took a long time dying.

Vincent is credited with the power to fight winter frost, hence his patronage of wine.

Left A depiction of the Martyrdom of St Vincent *(French manuscript illumination, 15th century).*

LUCY

YET ANOTHER VICTIM OF THE DIOCLETIAN PERSECUTION, LUCY WAS BELIEVED TO HAVE BEEN RESCUED BY THE HOLY SPIRIT. SHE IS REMEMBERED FOR THE MIRACULOUS RECOVERY OF HER EYES.

KEY FACTS
Virgin martyr
DATES: *d. AD 304*
BIRTH PLACE: *Syracuse, Sicily*
PATRON: *Against eye afflictions and throat infections*
FEAST DAY: *13 December*
EMBLEM: *Disembodied eyes, usually on a platter*

Lucy lost her father when she was a child but was, by all accounts, a resolute, devout young Sicilian. She had a loving mother, yet Lucy kept secret her Christian faith and her vow of virginity.

Her mother, Eutychia, was a wealthy noblewoman from Syracuse. She followed tradition by betrothing her adolescent daughter to a local youth. This expectation made Lucy confess her faith and she invited her mother to accompany her on a pilgrimage to the tomb of St Agatha. The two women prayed at this shrine and Eutychia was cured of haemorrhages from which she suffered. Grateful and convinced of Lucy's faith, she released the girl from the betrothal. But the young man was furious at the rejection of his marriage offer, and reported Lucy to the authorities who promptly arrested her.

MARTYRDOM

The persecution by the Emperor Diocletian was famous for its zeal in attacking Christianity, with many of its followers perishing.

The emperor sentenced Lucy to be taken to a brothel. However, it was said that the girl became immovable. Neither a gang of strong men nor a team of oxen could shift her. She had been filled by the Holy Spirit, making her miraculously heavy.

Her wardens could not lift her to take her to the stake for burning. So instead, it is claimed, they tore out her eyes and threw them on a platter. Lucy calmly

Above St Lucy displays her eyes on a platter (A. Colza, 1513).

took hold of them and put them back in their sockets. Her sight was magically restored. Frustrated by the failure of their cruel methods in persuading the saint to abandon her faith or her virginity, the soldiers beheaded the girl.

In many paintings, Lucy holds the platter bearing her eyes. Otherwise her eyes are dangling from a sprig of leaves or on her clothes. She has long been connected with light, partly because of the story of her eyes, and also because her name is linked to the Latin word for "light", *lux*.

Lucy is remembered in Sweden on the shortest day of the year with festivals at which young girls carry candles in her memory. She is likewise venerated in her birthplace, Sicily.

Below Detail of St Lucy resisting a team of oxen in front of the Judge Paschasius (Bartolo di Fredi, c. 1380).

PANTALEON

ONCE AMBITIOUS AND WORLDLY, PANTALEON ABANDONED A SUCCESSFUL CAREER IN MEDICINE TO LIVE "IN IMITATION OF CHRIST" AND WAS EVENTUALLY MARTYRED FOR HIS FAITH.

KEY FACTS
Martyr saint
DATES: *d.c.AD 305*
BIRTH PLACE: *Nicomedia (now Izmit, Turkey)*
PATRON OF: *Doctors, midwives, a Holy Helper*
FEAST DAY: *27 July*
EMBLEM: *Olive branch*

The Eastern Orthodox Church honours this saint as the "Great Martyr and Wonder Worker". (In the Greek language, Pantaleon means "all compassionate".) However, although his cult was well established in the East and West from an early date, there are no surviving authentic particulars of Pantaleon's life, which has become the subject of legends.

It is thought that he was the son of a pagan father, but was brought up as a Christian by his mother. He studied medicine and later practised as a doctor in Nicomedia (now Izmit) in Turkey, eventually gaining the important position of physician to the Emperor Galerius Maximianus.

However, being young and carefree, as well as ambitious and successful, Pantaleon abandoned his faith to enjoy the worldly pleasures of the royal palace. Fortunately, one of his friends from his former Christian life, Hermolaos, persistently reminded him of the truth of the Christian faith. When Emperor Diocletian came to power and started his fierce campaign of terror against Christians, Pantaleon realized where his feelings and loyalties lay. He distributed his wealth among the poor, treated the sick without receiving payment, and changed his life to one of discipline and austerity in imitation of Christ.

CAPTURE AND TORTURE

Other doctors, who had long envied Pantaleon for his success at court, took the opportunity to denounce him to the authorities.

Above *The church of St Pantaleon (AD 966–80) in Köln, Germany.*

He was arrested with Hermolaos and two other friends. The other three men were all executed, but the emperor, reluctant to lose a good doctor, begged Pantaleon to deny his faith. He refused, and his statement of faith was reinforced when he miraculously cured a cripple during his trial.

According to the stories, six types of torture were devised for Pantaleon. He was thrown into deep water to drown, then burning lead was poured over him. They tried to burn him, and they set wild beasts upon him. Then they turned him on a wheel and thrust a sword through his throat. But no matter what mode of torture was employed, Pantaleon was miraculously protected from harm, suffering no wounds and feeling no pain. When at last his tormentors beheaded him, it is said that milk flowed from his veins and the olive tree to which he had been tied burst into fruit.

In Ravello, southern Italy, a reputed relic of St Pantaleon's blood allegedly liquefies every year on his feast day.

Above *A fresco of St Pantaleon from Macedonia (12th century). Scarcely remembered now in the West, St Pantaleon is still venerated in the East, and many legends and miracles are associated with this martyr.*

LUCIAN OF ANTIOCH

THE MAN WHO ESTABLISHED THE IMPORTANT SCHOOL OF THEOLOGY IN ANTIOCH MADE AN AUTHORITATIVE TRANSLATION OF THE OLD TESTAMENT INTO GREEK BEFORE HIS MARTYRDOM.

KEY FACTS
Martyr saint
DATES: *d.AD 312*
BIRTH PLACE: *Samosata, Syria*
FEAST DAY: *7 January (West)*
EMBLEM: *Bishop's vestments, dolphins*

Orphaned at the age of 12, Lucian had Christian parents, who it is thought may have been martyred. He became the student of a famous teacher, Macarius of Edessa. After baptism, Lucian adopted a strictly ascetic life.

TEACHER AND SCHOLAR

His routine of disciplined habits allowed Lucian to write and study. He became a teacher, and is believed to be the man who established the school of theology in Antioch, which at that time was a significant Christian centre. One of his students was Arius, whose followers were sometimes known as Lucianists and who became the founder of Arianism.

Lucian is also known to have made an important translation of the Old Testament from Hebrew into Greek. His version, which corrected misleading translations in common use at the time, stressed the importance of maintaining the literal sense of the texts. His complete edition of the Bible, known as *Lucian Recension*, was used by St Jerome during his work on the *Vulgate*, and St John Chrysostom also regarded it as an authoritative text. Surviving manuscripts confirm this respect, and one such text, the Arundelian, is in the British Museum.

ORTHODOXY OR HERESY?

Lucian lived at a time of conflict within the Church in Antioch. Three successive bishops were hostile to his teachings, and for some years he was excluded from major meetings of Christian leaders. However, it seems that he otherwise enjoyed wide popular support. The people respected him for his great learning as well as admiring his noble character. He was later restored to office.

PRISON AND MARTYRDOM

During an outbreak of Christian persecution, Lucian was arrested and taken to Nicomedia, where he faced the Roman official Maximin Daza. He was thrown into prison, but, despite brutal treatment, his reputation for dignity and courage grew during the nine years he spent there. When dragged before the authorities for interrogation, he would always reply simply "I am a Christian".

At last, because he would not renounce his faith, his diet was reduced to sacrificial cake that had been dedicated to pagan idols. This he refused to eat. Some say he starved to death, but others relate that he was tortured and then beheaded. One legend even claimed he was flung into the sea and drowned, but that dolphins carried his body to shore where it was collected by his followers.

Lucian's relics were taken to Drepanum, where on the first anniversary of the saint's death, St John Chrysostom preached a tribute to this much-admired scholar and martyr.

Left The remains of the Roman Emperor Diocletian's palace at Nicomedia (now Izmit) in Turkey. Lucian suffered during Diocletian's persecution of Christians.

HELEN

THE MOTHER OF EMPEROR CONSTANTINE WAS AN ELDERLY WOMAN WHEN SHE CONVERTED. AN ANGEL IS SAID TO HAVE HELPED HER IDENTIFY THE TRUE CROSS WHILE SHE WAS VISITING THE HOLY LAND.

KEY FACTS
Mother of Constantine,
finder of the True Cross
DATES: *c.AD 250–330*
BIRTH PLACE: *Drepanum (later*
Helenopolis, in modern-day
north-west Turkey)
PATRON OF: *Archaeologists*
FEAST DAY: *18 August (West)*
EMBLEM: *Crown, cross*

Helen came from humble origins, but she made a grand marriage and gave birth to a great son. According to tradition, she was born in Drepanum (later renamed Helenopolis after her, by her son Constantine) and her father was an innkeeper. Her husband, Constantius Chlorus, a Roman general, divorced her when he became Emperor of Rome in AD 292, but their son greatly honoured her.

FINDING THE TRUE CROSS
When in her sixties, Helen made a pilgrimage to Jerusalem. She had converted to Christianity by this time. Her son, who was by then emperor, had organized diggings to uncover the holy sites of Jesus and the apostles.

It is told that Helen was at the hill of Calvary, where foundations were being dug for the church of the Holy Sepulchre, when three

Left St Helen *(Altobello Meloni, 15th century).*

crosses were excavated. A woman with a terminal illness was touched by each of the crosses, and the True Cross cured her, thus revealing its sacred nature.

Relics of the Cross were taken to Rome, where they were housed in the Basilica of Santa Croce, built for the purpose. The Holy Stairs – allegedly the marble steps excavated from the hall of Pontius Pilate where Christ's trial was held – were also moved to Rome.

Helen was renowned for her generosity and work among prisoners and the poor, and she founded churches in both Palestine and Rome.

CONSTANTINE THE GREAT

Some biographies of Constantine claim his mother, Helen, was his father's paramour, not a wife. Though his father was emperor, Constantine still had to fight hard to win leadership of the Roman Empire. His cause was doubtless helped by his diplomatic skills. Although he promoted Christianity after his conversion, he was reluctant to cause strife in a predominantly pagan Rome. As emperor, he founded Constantinople (now Istanbul) on the site of the old city of Byzantium, which in time became the centre of the Christian world.

Right Emperor Constantine and St Helen with the True Cross *(fresco, c.8th century).*

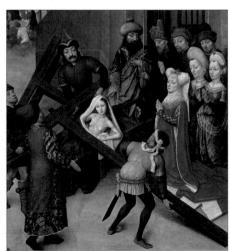

Above St Helena and the Miracle of the True Cross *(attr. to Simon Marmion, 15th century).*

PACHOMIUS

A COMPETENT ADMINISTRATOR, THIS FORMER ROMAN SOLDIER WAS HIGHLY INFLUENTIAL IN ESTABLISHING ORDERLY COMMUNAL LIFE FOR HERMITS IN THE REGION OF UPPER EGYPT.

KEY FACTS
Founder of the first monasteries
DATES: c.*AD 290–346*
BIRTH PLACE: *Esna,*
Upper Egypt
FEAST DAY: *9 May (West)*
EMBLEM: *Appearance of a hermit*

Life in the Roman army prepared Pachomius well for the path he chose to follow. Born to heathen parents in Egypt, he was conscripted into the Roman army, where he fought under Constantine the Great. He became a Christian after his return home, and immediately went to live in the wilderness, there putting himself under the guidance of an old hermit named Palemon.

Pachomius lived near the River Nile and became part of a small community of other ascetics committed to the austere life of a recluse. An angel is said to have visited Pachomius after a few years and told him to establish a monastery in the desert. It seems this Desert Father preferred the life of the community to that of the solitary. He was concerned, too, that some of his fellow hermits were extreme in their behaviour and that they were running the risk of madness from starvation and hardship.

Above This Byzantine mosaic includes Pachomius' name in Latin in the design (12th century).

The monks and nuns took vows of chastity, poverty and obedience, and regulations regarding diet and prayer were strict but humane. Fanaticism was outlawed and meditation and prayer were supervised. Members learnt by heart passages from the Psalms and other books of the Bible. Pachomius acted as an army general might do in running the monasteries. Monks were commanded to move from one house to another, superiors were put in charge of each house, and accounts were presented every year.

The order he founded was known as the Tabennisiots, after a place near his first monastery. Pachomius' manuscripts have not survived, but his Rule was translated into Latin by St Jerome, and this influenced Sts Basil the Great and Benedict, both of whom founded great monastic orders based on St Pachomius' methods.

St Athanasius the Aconite, patriarch of Alexandria, was a friend of Pachomius and visited the monk in his monastery at Dendera, near the Nile, where Pachomius lived out his life. The Eastern Orthodox Church holds this remarkable man in high veneration.

FOUNDING MONASTERIES

His life in the army had taught Pachomius about the organization of a dedicated community, and he also had a flair for administration. After his first monastery was founded in AD 320, he established nine others for men and two nunneries for women, and wrote rules for living in these communities.

Right St Pachomius (16th century). The saint, remembered for building the first monasteries, is shown in this fresco to be casting his saintly light on the construction of a grand tower.

ANTONY OF EGYPT

THIS SAINT IS OFTEN REGARDED AS THE FATHER OF MONASTICISM, AND WAS KNOWN FOR HIS HEALINGS, BUT IT IS HIS LIFE OF SOLITUDE, PRAYER AND GENTLENESS THAT HAS HAD THE MOST LASTING IMPACT.

KEY FACTS
Desert Father, ascetic
DATES: *AD 251–356*
BIRTH PLACE: *Coma, Egypt*
PATRON OF: *Skin diseases, domestic animals and pets, basket-makers*
FEAST DAY: *17 January*
EMBLEM: *Pig, bell*

The popular view of saintliness is embodied by St Antony of Egypt. He was not tempted by worldly goods or comfort, he did no harm to others, he was not too proud to undertake humble work, and he spent his life in prayer.

SOLITUDE AND PRAYER

Born into a respectable Christian family in Coma in Upper Egypt, Antony was given a narrow education. When his parents died, he was 20 and heir to a considerable estate. But he recalled the words of Christ, "Go, sell what thou hast,

Left St Antony in a stained glass from Suffolk, England (17th century). He was once a swineherd and St Antony's cross can be seen on his cloak.

and give it to the poor, and thou shalt have treasure in Heaven." He gave away his land and wealth, keeping only enough for the care of his younger sister, and lived among local ascetics. Then for 20 years, from AD 286 to AD 306, he took to the desert, where he lived a life of complete solitude and extreme austerity, seeking the love of God in prayer and meditation.

When he was 54, Antony was asked to leave his hermitage and organize some nearby ascetics into a monastic order. Back on his mountain, the hermit cultivated a garden and wove baskets. A follower, Marcarius, guarded him from curious onlookers.

Toward the end of his life, Antony visited Alexandria to comfort persecuted Christians and refute Arianism. He was, by now, famous for his wisdom and miracles; crowds rushed to see him and many were converted.

Sufferers from ergotism (also known as "St Antony's Fire") visited his shrine at La Motte in France, where the Order of Hospitallers of Saint Antony was founded *c.*1100, to seek a cure.

Left The central panel of The Temptation of St Anthony *(Hieronymus Bosch, c.1505).*

BASIL THE GREAT

VENERATED FOR HIS ROBUST DEFENCE OF THE FAITH, THIS DOCTOR OF THE CHURCH WAS ALSO AN IMPORTANT FIGURE IN ESTABLISHING MONASTIC RULES DEDICATED TO CHARITABLE WORK AND POVERTY.

KEY FACTS

Doctor of the Eastern Church
DATES: *c.AD 330–79*
BIRTH PLACE: *Cappadocia, Turkey*
PATRON OF: *Russia, monks of the Eastern Churches*
FEAST DAY: *2 January (with St Gregory of Nazianzus)*
EMBLEM: *Bishop's vestments, often pictured with other early Doctors of the Church*

Basil's extensive writings reveal a humorous, tender person, yet he proved unyielding in his fight for orthodoxy.

He was born in Cappadocia, one of ten children in an extraordinary family: his grandmother, both parents, and three siblings were all destined for sainthood.

On returning from studies in Constantinople and Athens, where he had become good friends with Gregory of Nazianzus, he travelled widely, to Palestine, Egypt, Syria and Mesopotamia, studying the religious life, before taking up life as a hermit in Cappadocia. His brother joined him there in a life of contemplation and preaching.

Basil established the first monastery in Asia Minor, instigating a brotherhood of hard labour, charitable work and communal routine, a system that he believed better served God and his faithful than did solitary asceticism. His rule, unchanged, is followed by monks today in the Eastern Orthodox Church, and forms the basis of orders dedicated to him.

BATTLING ARIANISM

During Basil's lifetime, a schism threatened the Church, caused by the popular teachings of Arius, which denied the divinity of Jesus.

The harsh activities of the Arian Emperor Valens against traditionalism brought Basil back to Caesarea to protect his community from attack. Valens was too afraid of Basil's reputation to act against him, and withdrew from Caesarea, but he continued

***Above** An icon from Moscow shows St Basil wearing the* omophor *vestment of an Eastern Orthodox bishop and holding a copy of the Gospels.*

to promote Arianism elsewhere. Basil preached daily to huge crowds and produced numerous texts on belief that remain in use in the Eastern Orthodox Church.

During a period of drought, he built hospitals and soup kitchens where his monks served the poor. But anxious that the faith might be waning in the east, he increased his preaching, emphasizing the Church's beliefs. His lessons were conveyed everywhere both by texts and through word of mouth.

In AD 378, Valens died and was succeeded by his nephew, Gratian, who discouraged Arianism. As Basil himself lay dying a year later,

he was confident that, with the emperor on his side, orthodoxy would prevail.

Christians, pagans and Jews all mourned the "father and protector" of Caesarea, while the Church honoured St Basil for keeping the faith alive. He is one of the great Doctors of the Church.

***Below** An 18th-century altarpiece in St Peter's Basilica in Rome shows St Basil defiantly celebrating mass in the presence of the Emperor Valens.*

BARBARA

THE LEGEND OF ST BARBARA IS A ROMANTIC ONE ABOUT A BRAVE AND BEAUTIFUL GIRL WHO REFUSES ALL SUITORS FOR CHRIST. HER CULTUS WAS POPULAR IN FRANCE DURING THE MIDDLE AGES.

KEY FACTS
Virgin martyr
DATES: *Unknown*
BIRTH PLACE: *Unknown*
PATRON OF: *Gunners, artillery, dying people, miners*
FEAST DAY: *Formerly 4 December, but removed from Roman calendar in 1969*
EMBLEM: *Tower*

It is highly unlikely that this saint ever existed: although she allegedly lived in the 3rd century, nothing was written about her until the 7th. She was officially de-canonized in 1969.

According to the *Golden Legend*, Barbara was the daughter of a pagan, who locked her in a tower so that no man could see her. But her beauty was so renowned that men still came to court her. When Barbara became a Christian, her father was so furious that he tried to kill her, but she miraculously escaped.

Above St Barbara (Flemish manuscript illumination, 1475).

Eventually she was handed over to a judge, who condemned her to death and ordered her father to carry out the deed. This he did, but he was immediately struck by lightning and died.

This is the reason that Barbara is regarded as a patron of those in danger of sudden death, originally from lightning, later from cannon-balls, gunfire or mines.

CYRIL OF JERUSALEM

THE LESSONS OF ST CYRIL FOR THOSE SEEKING BAPTISM ARE SO PROFOUND, AND HIS FIGHT FOR THE TRUE FAITH SO EARNEST, THAT HE IS HONOURED AS A DOCTOR OF THE CHURCH.

KEY FACTS
Doctor of the Church
DATES: *c.AD 315–86*
BIRTH PLACE: *Jerusalem*
FEAST DAY: *18 March*
EMBLEM: *Bishop's gown*

St Cyril was a clear thinker and an excellent teacher. But it was his misfortune to live during a time of schism among the Eastern Christian communities, when the ideas of the unorthodox Arians were gaining ground against the traditionalist concept of the Holy Trinity – the threefold godhead of Father, Son and Holy Spirit.

Cyril was born and educated in Jerusalem. After becoming a priest, his first assignment, from St Maximus, was to train converts preparing for baptism. His lessons of faith were – and indeed still are – much admired, and they brought him prestige and high office.

Left The Church of the Holy Sepulchre in Jerusalem where St Cyril was bishop during the 4th century AD. This scene has scarcely changed since.

When he first became Bishop of Jerusalem in AD 349, strange lights were said to fill the sky over the city. But during the 35 years Cyril served as a bishop, he spent much of his life in hot dispute with the dominant Arians. He was first exiled in AD 357, and although he was recalled two years later, he was banished twice more and spent a total of 16 years in exile.

However, in AD 381, Cyril took part in the First Council of Constantinople, which gave official endorsement to the concept of the Trinity. St Cyril was made a Doctor of the Church in 1882.

GREGORY OF NAZIANZUS

THE INSPIRED PREACHING AND WRITING OF ST GREGORY HELPED
TO UNIFY THE EASTERN ORTHODX CHURCHES IN TIMES OF STRIFE.
AS A RESULT HE WAS MADE A DOCTOR OF THE CHURCH.

KEY FACTS
*Doctor of the Eastern
Orthodox Church*
DATES: *AD 329–89*
BIRTH PLACE: *Arianzus, south-
west Cappadocia, Turkey*
FEAST DAY: *2 January*
EMBLEM: *Bishop's gown*

This shy, diffident poet-priest was the son of wealthy parents, Gregory, Bishop of Nazianzus and his wife Nonna, who were able to give him the best education. He attended the renowned theological school at Caesarea and continued his studies first at Alexandria and then at the University of Athens, where he rekindled his youthful friendship with St Basil the Great.

RELUCTANT PRIEST

Together, the two friends formed a common resolve to live a contemplative life, and when Basil set up a retreat in Pontus (now Turkey), Gregory joined him. Together they wrote the Monastic Rules.

After two years of the contemplative life, Gregory returned to Nazianzus. His father, now elderly, was not happy with his son's decision to live as a monk, and resolved to have him home. In AD 361, the bishop forced his son to be ordained as a priest.

Neither did his friend leave him in peace. Basil, who had by then become Archbishop of Caesarea, had Gregory consecrated as Bishop of Sasima, most probably to maintain his own influence in what was a disputed area. The place, however, was a hostile border settlement and Gregory spent little time there. The whole affair brought about a quarrel between the pair, from which their friendship never fully recovered.

After the death of his parents, Gregory, who had always desired the contemplative life, escaped briefly to a monastery in Seleucia.

Above These images depict the visions seen by the Old Testament prophet Ezekiel. They form part of The Homilies of St Gregory, *an illuminated manuscript that is held in Paris (9th century).*

AGAINST HERESY

Five years later, in 379, Gregory was recalled to serve the Christian community of Constantinople in their battle for orthodoxy. Church officials were determined to use Gregory's oratorial talents in their dispute with Arianism.

The heresy had been so successful in Constantinople that there was no longer an Orthodox Church active there, and Gregory was obliged to use his house to hold meetings. Here, he preached five discourses on the Holy Trinity. These teachings helped ensure that orthodoxy was confirmed at the First Council of

Constantinople in AD 381. For a brief, unhappy period he was Bishop of Constantinople, but differences of opinion with the Eastern bishops led him to resign.

PEACE AT LAST

Gregory spent his last years in priestly duties in Nazianzus and in retreat. Many of his letters survive, as does an autobiography and some religious poetry.

After his death aged 60, St Gregory's relics were translated to Constantinople and later to Rome. He is one of the great Eastern Doctors of the Church alongside Sts John Chrysostom and Basil the Great.

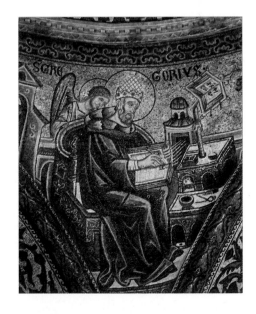

Above St Gregory of Nazianzus, overseen by an angel while working at his desk, in a mosaic in the second dome of the Basilica San Marco, Venice (c. 1350).

AMBROSE

THIS POPULAR BISHOP OF MILAN BECAME A KEY COMBATANT IN THE STRUGGLE AGAINST THE ARIAN HERESY. HE ALSO WROTE IMPORTANT TEXTS ON CHRISTIAN ETHICS AND INTERPRETATION OF THE BIBLE.

A vigorous intellect, energy and charm helped Ambrose in the murky political world he encountered as Bishop of Milan.

He was the son of a noble Roman family, and legend tells that, when he was child, a swarm of bees settled on him, which was deemed to symbolize his future eloquence (hence his patronage).

He studied law, Greek, rhetoric and poetry before becoming consular prefect of Liguria and Aemilia, with headquarters in Milan. He was a gifted administrator and diplomatic leader – and the citizens trusted him.

KEY FACTS
One of the four great Latin Doctors of the Western Church
DATES: *AD 339–97*
BIRTH PLACE: *Trier, Germany*
PATRON OF: *Bees, beekeepers and those who work with wax*
FEAST DAY: *7 December (West)*
EMBLEM: *Whip, to symbolize his fight against heresy*

Left Enthroned Ambrose *(Alvise Vivarini, 1503).*

Then Ambrose took to studying Christianity. In AD 374, when the bishop of Milan died, he attended the council meeting to elect a successor. Ambrose was not a follower of Arianism, a sect that was strong in the Milan area, and gave a speech favouring orthodox beliefs. To his great surprise – he was not even baptized – he was elected bishop and was in office within a week.

TACKLING THE HERETICS

The new bishop took charge of a weak Church. The empire, too, was stricken by battles for supremacy between East and West.

The greatest demonstration of his moral strength was shown after the Massacre of Thessalonica in AD 390. The governor there had been assassinated and, in retribution, Theodosius, Emperor of the eastern Roman Empire, ordered thousands of citizens to be killed. Ambrose was horrified. He faced Theodosius and reminded him that God was more important than the state, and that even the emperor must submit to holy law. Contrite, Theodosius made a public penance for his savage act.

Left The Emperor Theodosius and Saint Ambrose *(Peter Paul Rubens, 17th century).*

AGATHA

ALTHOUGH LITTLE IS ACTUALLY KNOWN ABOUT THIS SAINT, HER ALLEGED BRAVERY IN THE FACE OF HORRIFIC TORTURE AND DEATH ENSURED HER A WIDESPREAD FOLLOWING IN MEDIEVAL TIMES.

Although there is some evidence that a virgin martyr named Agatha died in Catania in the first years of the 4th century, little is known about this saint. However, her memory persists and she is patron of Catania.

Her legend recounts that her parents were Christians from the nobility who openly refused to offer sacrifices to pagan gods. The local consul Quintinian, who tried unsuccessfully to seduce Agatha, raised a campaign against all Christians, and the young girl was arrested. As she approached the consul, she prayed, "Jesus Christ, Lord of all, Thou seest my heart… I am thy sheep: make me worthy to overcome the devil."

Her persecutors were aware that virginity was important to their Christian victims, so Agatha was sent to a brothel. It is said that her faith and piety shone from her, and no man dared approach her.

MUTILATION AND DEATH

Instead, she was taken away to be tortured. Agatha was not afraid of martyrdom because it meant she would soon join Christ. Quintinian devised a mutilation suited to horrify a beautiful young girl. His henchman pierced and severed Agatha's breasts.

St Peter is said to have visited Agatha and restored her breasts. However, she was then forced to walk across hot coals and shards of glass. But as she took her first step, Mount Etna erupted and an earthquake shook the earth. The watching crowd screamed for her release, convinced her God was

Above This marble altarpiece portrays the coronation of St Agatha in heaven (15th century).

KEY FACTS
Virgin martyr
DATES: *Unknown*
BIRTH PLACE: *Catania or Palermo in Sicily*
PATRON OF: *Protection from breast disease, volcanoes and fire; jewellers, nurses, bell founders, Catania*
FEAST DAY: *5 February*
EMBLEM: *Mutilated breasts, often carried on a dish*

punishing them all. Quintinian stopped the torture, but quietly starved her to death instead.

St Agatha is often the subject of paintings illustrating her mutilation. The resemblance in shape of bells to breasts is the reason for her patronage of bell founders.

Below Saint Agatha (Francesco Guarino, 17th century).

MARTIN OF TOURS

THE SON OF A MILITARY MAN, MARTIN JOINED THE ARMY BUT CHOSE INSTEAD TO BE A "SOLDIER OF CHRIST". HE FOLLOWED HIS FAITH WITH ENERGY AND CONVICTION.

This saint is traditionally commemorated as having led a life of bravery as a "soldier of God". In fact, his first career was in the army – following his pagan father's footsteps – but he came to believe that war was incompatible with his commitment to Christ. When accused of cowardice, he offered to stand unarmed between the opposing sides, but was instead discharged from the army.

Martin became known for his charity as well as moral courage. One famous legend recounts that as a soldier riding to Amiens in bitterly cold weather, he saw a poor man dressed in rags. Filled with compassion for the man's plight, he cut his heavy army cloak in two and wrapped the man in one half. That night, as he slept, Jesus appeared to him wearing that half of the cloak.

Below Saint Martin Sharing His Cloak with a Poor Man *(Domenico Ghirlandaio and workshop, 15th century).*

Above The Mass of St Martin of Tours *(Eustache Le Sueur, 1654).*

MONK AND BISHOP

For ten years, Martin lived at Ligugé, a plot of land given to him by Hilary, the Bishop of Poitiers. Originally living a solitary life, Martin was soon joined by others, and founded a monastery there – the first one in Gaul. Then, in AD 372, at the acclamation of clergy and people, he was elected as Bishop of Tours.

After his ordination, he continued to live as a monk, moving to a solitary place, Marmoutier, where he later founded one of several other monasteries.

Martin travelled around his parish on foot and by donkey, preaching over a wide area with a desire to see the conversion of rural areas. He destroyed heathen temples and sacred trees and performed many miracles, notably healing lepers. It is said that he even raised a dead man to life.

He became involved in many doctrinal disputes. In AD 384, when some bishops appealed to the Roman authorities to execute local heretics, Martin begged (in vain) for their lives, claiming banishment was sufficient. Such a forgiving nature ensured his popularity into old age. A mausoleum marks his grave at Tours.

PELAGIA THE PENITENT

THIS BEAUTIFUL AND TALENTED ACTRESS ABANDONED HER FORMER
LIFE AND WEALTH TO BECOME A CHRISTIAN. SHE LIVED THE REST OF
HER LIFE AS A RECLUSIVE HERMIT DISGUISED AS A MAN.

KEY FACTS
Penitent
DATES: *5th century*
BIRTH PLACE: *Antioch*
PATRON OF: *Actresses*
FEAST DAY: *8 October*
EMBLEM: *Hermit*

In the 5th century, St John Chrysostom wrote about a glamorous harlot of Antioch who repented and became a nun. The story of Pelagia the Penitent seems to follow this tale but it comes with embellishments.

Pelagia was a beautiful and immensely wealthy woman as well as an actress, which was considered a disgraceful profession.

She liked to sway through the promenades of Antioch, dressed in marvellous clothes to flaunt her attributes. A retinue of admirers followed in her wake. One day as she passed a solemn group of bishops attending a service given by bishop Nonnus of Edessa, a leading Christian, the men turned their backs on her. But Nonnus himself stopped preaching and admired the lovely woman. He was troubled that she was clearly so successful at her chosen yet despised profession, while he felt he had failed as bishop to his Christian flock.

PELAGIA'S CONVERSION

Nonnus prayed all through the night, then the next morning went to attend to his duties at the cathedral. Pelagia, who had heard his preaching, followed him and begged to be baptized. She was given instruction by a deaconess and accepted into the Christian community. After her baptism, she gave away all her possessions and disappeared from Antioch. She

crept off and, dressed as a man, she took up the life of a hermit on the Mount of Olives in Jerusalem.

Pelagia was forgotten by all her old companions although some Christians visited her. A deacon, known as James, was said to have sought an interview with the "beardless recluse", and afterwards wrote down her story. Only at her death did people realize that this hermit was not only a woman, but one with an infamous reputation in the city of Antioch.

The legend has been seen as a fine example of penitence. Others say it was written by a male hermit who longed for a female counterpart in his harsh life.

Pelagia's story has remained a popular one, and has been told in a number of versions over the centuries – from the fourth all the way to the thirteenth. Her name appears in many ports and villages around the Mediterranean Sea.

Right Sts Pelagia and Euphemia in a mosaic from San Apollinare Nuovo, Ravenna, Italy (AD 561).

NICHOLAS OF MYRA

LEGENDS ABOUT THE PATRON OF RUSSIA CREDIT ST NICHOLAS WITH BEING A MIRACLE WORKER BLESSED WITH THE VIRTUES OF KINDNESS AND GENEROSITY – ESPECIALLY TOWARD CHILDREN.

This saint is famous for his role as Father Christmas. The fact that he is patron of children may explain this status. Alternatively, the reason might lie in the legend that St Nicholas once found three dead children hidden in a brine tub and brought them miraculously back to life. There is also the story of his rescue of three young girls doomed to prostitution through poverty. As a gift, St Nicholas threw three bags of gold into their window, thus providing the girls with marriage dowries.

There is evidence that a bishop of Myra, named Nicholas, did live in the 4th century AD, but little else is known about him. Some claimed St Nicholas attended the Church's first General Council in

Above This fresco shows St Nicholas saving three condemned knights from death (Giotto School, c.1300–5).

Below Saint Nicholas Protecting the Sailors (Vitale da Bologna, 14th century). He is patron saint of sailors.

KEY FACTS
Identified with Santa Claus
DATES: *4th century AD*
BIRTH PLACE: *Possibly Patara, Lycia (modern-day Turkey)*
PATRON OF: *Children, brides, unmarried girls, Russia, travellers, sailors, maritime navigators*
FEAST DAY: *6 December*
EMBLEM: *Three balls or bags of gold, purse, anchor, ship*

Nicaea in AD 325. Or he may have been martyred before Constantine legalized Christianity in AD 313.

A PEOPLE'S SAINT

Despite his lost life story, St Nicholas has been, since early Christian history, a popular saint. His image can be found all over Russia and the Christian Middle East. Churches everywhere are dedicated in his name.

His many legends depict a strong, chivalrous man. He rescued three sailors from drowning, and saved three condemned men from execution. Sailors faced with a storm called upon his name, and it is said St Nicholas appeared at the shore and calmed the waves.

His physical strength was revealed as a newborn, when he sprang to his feet and stood firm. And as a small boy, he showed deep devotion, listening attentively to the sermons of the local bishop, his uncle.

Italians stole his relics in 1095 and gave them to the church in Bari, where they remain to this day. Europeans carried his name to the New World. Linguists have observed that Dutch settlers in the USA called him "Sinte Klaas". Following European tradition, they would have given presents on his feast day, thus starting the Santa Claus tradition.

BLAISE

KNOWN FOR HIS KINDNESS AND FOR HIS MEDICAL SKILLS, BLAISE
WAS SOUGHT BY BELIEVERS TO INTERCEDE NOT ONLY FOR THEIR
OWN HEALING BUT ALSO FOR THEIR PETS AND FARM ANIMALS.

KEY FACTS
Martyr saint
DATES: *4th century AD*
BIRTH PLACE: *Sebaste, Armenia*
PATRON OF: *Doctors, farmers,
wool trade, laryngologists, builders,
veterinarians, a Holy Helper*
FEAST DAY: *3 February*
EMBLEM: *Wool-comb,
two crossed candles*

Although no historical details of his life exist, the stories of Blaise's healings have made him popular and his feast day is still celebrated in some churches.

It is said that Blaise was born into a wealthy, Christian home in the 4th century AD. Blaise became Bishop of Sebaste in Armenia while he was still young, but he lived during the reign of Emperor Licinius, a time of severe persecution of Christians.

Warned by his brethren that his life was in danger, Blaise fled to the hills, where he remained isolated from his community, and where, allegedly, wild animals would turn to Blaise when they were ill or hurt and he would heal them.

STORIES OF HEALINGS

Among many stories is one of a countrywoman who came to the saint's cave with her small son who was choking to death on a fishbone. Blaise touched the child's throat, the bone was dislodged, and the boy survived.

Eventually, Blaise was arrested. It is told that as he was marched off to jail, he passed a wolf loping off with a pig in its mouth, while nearby a poor woman wept at the loss of her animal. Blaise ordered the wolf to drop its prey and was instantly obeyed. The grateful woman later brought the prisoner food, and a candle to light his cell. Indeed, different traditions have varied tales of St Blaise, but all tell of farmers calling on him for help with their sickly animals. Water with the blessing of St Blaise is given to sick cattle.

PATRONAGE

The saint is also associated with mending sore throats, and some churches celebrate the Blessing of the Throat on his feast day. The priest ties ribbons to two candles, then touches the candle ends to the throat of the sufferer, saying, "May the Lord deliver you from the evil of the throat, and from all other evil."

Perhaps Blaise's torturers knew of his bond with animals because, before beheading him, along with numerous other tortures, they combed his flesh with an iron wool-comb. In time the wool comb came to be his emblem, and he became patron of the wool trade. For a long time, his feast day was celebrated with a procession in Bradford, once the centre of the English wool business.

St Blaise's cult is not known before the 8th century, but he became one of the most popular saints of the Middle Ages, most probably due to his association with miraculous cures. He was called upon to help diseased people and animals, and his name lives on in the village of St Blazey in Cornwall, England.

St Blaise also enjoys an international cultus. He is the patron saint of Dubrovnic, and in Spain he is venerated under the name of San Blas; in Italy he is known as San Biagio. He is one of the Fourteen Holy Helpers.

Below A statue of St Blaise in Dubrovnik, Croatia (15th century).

Above Saint Blaise *(Giovanni Battista Tiepolo, 1740). His bishop's vestments give no hint of his hardships as a hermit.*

JEROME

THE GREATEST BIBLICAL SCHOLAR OF HIS TIME WAS VENERATED FOR HIS AUTHORITATIVE TRANSLATION OF THE BIBLE FROM THE ORIGINAL HEBREW AND GREEK VERSIONS INTO LATIN.

Numerous paintings of Jerome have created an abiding image of a lean old man, bent over his books in a remote cave. At his feet a large friendly lion keeps benevolent guard. But the reality was quite different.

Jerome seems to have been a man at war with himself. He longed to concentrate on his studies but also sought academic debate. A quick temper and impatient manner made this saint unpleasantly aggressive and

KEY FACTS
One of the four great Latin Doctors of the Western Church
DATES: *c.AD 341–420*
BIRTH PLACE: *Strido, Dalmatia (Balkans)*
PATRON OF: *Scholars, students, archaeologists, librarians, translators*
FEAST DAY: *30 September*
EMBLEM: *Bishop's hat, book, stone and lion*

Left St Jerome *(Theodoricus of Prague, 14th century). Often his symbol in art is a book.*

intolerant of his colleagues' ideas. Critics bemoaned his lack of Christian meekness and surfeit of sarcasm and unkindness.

EARLY LIFE

Jerome received a classical education and went on to study further in Rome. During this time he nursed an ambition to experience the world and in order to fulfil this ambition, the young man travelled widely and actively sought out teachers and further intellectual stimulation.

At this early stage in his life Jerome was not devout, being too interested in the literature and philosophy of the Greeks. After a headstrong dispute in Rome with colleagues, he felt impelled to leave the city and travelled again, this time with two friends touring eastern Europe.

However, a chance occurrence changed his life. All three men fell dangerously ill with a severe fever. The subsequent death of both his companions had a profound impact on Jerome, who

Left Saint Jerome in a Landscape *(Giovanni Battista Cima da Conegliano, c. 1500–1510).*

turned to the Christian faith. But his commitment to Christianity caused him great anguish.

He greatly enjoyed the company of women, and found too much pleasure in reading pagan Greek texts. Believing these joys would carry him away from God, he decided to abstain from them. To this end, Jerome went to live as a hermit in the desert where he could think and pray without distraction.

GREAT SCHOLAR
Somewhat against his will, he was ordained and sent back to Rome in AD 382. Pope Damasus I saw that this man would never do as a parish priest but believed his scholarship could serve well.

Jerome produced important texts about traditional dogma and monasticism, and expounded the virtue of celibacy. He wrote in praise of the Virgin Mary, asserting the view that she remained a virgin throughout her life.

Posterity honours him for translating the Bible from Greek and Hebrew into Latin. His version is known as the Vulgate or Authorized Bible. Jerome was the first scholar to make the distinction between the "true" texts and the dubious, or

"Show me, O Lord, Your mercy and delight my heart with it. Let me find you for whom I so long-ingly seek...
I am the sheep who wandered into the wilderness – seek after me and bring me home to your fold.

Amen"

PRAYER OF ST JEROME

Above Annunciation to Mary with the Saints Jerome and John the Baptist *(Francesco Raibolini, c.1448–1517).*

"apocryphal", texts. His work has proved invaluable to theologians ever since.

As was his wont, however, Jerome became embroiled in theological dispute, this time with the heretical Arians, about whom he wrote a scathing attack. And in the process it is possible he made one too many enemies.

SCANDAL AND FLIGHT
Jerome's promotion of a study group for girls and widows in Rome proved to be too risky. Soon rumour was rife that Jerome shared more than his religious teachings with the ladies. Despite protests of his innocence, he did not have the support of friends and was forced to flee.

Jerome travelled to Cyprus and Antioch where two Roman women, the widow Paula and her daughter, joined him. Together they went to Egypt, then returned to Bethlehem in the Holy Land.

Paula established three nunneries in Bethlehem, and she built a monastery for men which Jerome headed. Living in a cave nearby, he

continued to analyse scripture. Even from this remote spot, his sharp tongue aroused fury among fellow theologians. He went into hiding again, before returning to Bethlehem in AD 418.

By then Jerome was old and sickly. It is said he died with his head resting on the manger where baby Jesus was born. Jerome was buried under the Church of the Nativity in Bethlehem.

JEROME AND THE LION
A lion had crept into the monastery in Bethlehem and its presence was frightening the monks. But the animal was limping, and Jerome, realizing its distress, and impatient no doubt with the squeals of his colleagues, strode over and removed a thorn from the lion's paw. For the rest of his days, the lion padded along next to him. Perhaps a dumb beast suited the saint's social temperament better than could a human. After Jerome's death, the lion protected the monastery's domestic animals.

Above Saint Jerome Reading *(Rembrandt Harmensz van Rijn, 1634).*

JOHN CHRYSOSTOM

BOTH LOVED AND HATED FOR UPHOLDING CHRISTIAN PRINCIPLES, ST JOHN CHRYSOSTOM WAS A GREAT PREACHER, WHO ALSO PRODUCED PROFOUND INSIGHTS INTO SCRIPTURE.

KEY FACTS
Doctor, Eastern Orthodox Church
DATES: *AD 47–407*
BIRTH PLACE: *Antioch, Syria (site of modern-day Antakya, Turkey)*
PATRON OF: *Preaching, sacred oratory, Constantinople*
FEAST DAY: *13 September (West)*
EMBLEM: *Bishop's gown*

A man of high intellect, John Chrysostom knew how to touch the hearts of his listeners. A committed ascetic, he aroused fury among those churchmen who preferred ease and luxury to the simplicity of a devout life.

John grew up in the major Christian centre of Antioch (in Syria). After his father died, his mother brought him up as a Christian. He studied law, but opted instead for a religious life. After his baptism, *c.*AD 370, he retired to the desert.

For health reasons, he returned to Antioch where he was ordained a priest in AD 386. His eloquent preaching won him many followers in the city.

REFORM AND OPPOSITION

In AD 398, he was appointed Archbishop of Constantinople, and began to instigate moral reform. He dedicated church money to hospitals, forbade the clergy from keeping servants, and put idle monks to work.

It was not long before he faced opposition. Empress Eudoxia took his attacks on the morals at court as a personal affront, and Theophilus, Bishop of Alexandria, demanded that John be exiled from Constantinople.

He was briefly recalled, but then banished again a year later, and eventually died of exhaustion after he was forced to travel long distances on foot in bad weather.

Left Detail of St John Chrysostom from the Apse Mosaic, San Paolo fuori le Mura, Rome (Edward Burne-Jones, 19th century).

A RENOWNED TEACHER

St John Chrysostom is remembered for his preaching – his name means "golden mouth" in Greek. He emphasized literal interpretation and practical application of scripture and wrote treatises on the Psalms, St Matthew's Gospel and St Paul's Epistles. He is admired in the West, where he is one of the four Great Doctors of the Eastern Orthodox Church.

Right St John Chrysostom exiled by the Empress Eudoxia *(Benjamin Constant, 19th century).*

AUGUSTINE OF HIPPO

THIS INFLUENTIAL THINKER FROM NORTH AFRICA WAS THE ARCHITECT OF EARLY CHURCH DOCTRINE. HIS WRITINGS, *CITY OF GOD* AND *CONFESSIONS*, BECAME FAMOUS CHRISTIAN TEXTS.

KEY FACTS

One of the four great Latin Doctors of the Western Church, Bishop of Hippo
DATES: *AD 354–430*
BIRTH PLACE: *Tagaste (now in Algeria)*
PATRON OF: *Printers and theologians, brewers, against eye diseases*
FEAST DAY: *28 August*
EMBLEM: *Bishop's staff and mitre, dove, pen, shell, child*

As a young man of Roman Carthage, Augustine had considerable intellect and charm. His vivacity brought him, by the age of 20, a concubine and small son, Adeodatus. But he matured into a disciplined theologian and bishop, kindly towards his flock.

His pagan father ensured Augustine was well educated. His mother, St Monica, was a Christian but her son rejected her beliefs. Driven by ambition, he moved with his family from North Africa to Rome, and then to Milan. He was a restless man, searching for a vocation. His widowed mother insisted he send the

"O God our Father, who dost exhort us to pray, and who does grant what we ask, hear me, who am trembling in the darkness, and stretch forth Thy hand to me, hold forth Thy light before me, recall me from my wanderings, and may I be restored to myself and to Thee.

Amen."

PRAYER OF ST AUGUSTINE

Below St Augustine *(the Master of Grossgmain, c.1498).*

Above A view of St Augustine's Cathedral at Hippo Regius, a Roman town in Algeria.

concubine, his companion of 15 years, back to Africa. Shortly after this separation, Augustine claimed to hear a heavenly child's voice bearing a divine message.

CONVERSION

His subsequent conversion to Christianity, however, was marred by the emotional conflict between, on the one hand, his love of comfort and women, and on the other, the austerity demanded by his faith. These feelings are recorded in his autobiography, *Confessions*.

He and his son were baptized in AD 387 and, with a group of friends, retired to his estates in Africa. The group took vows of chastity, poverty and obedience, and undertook charitable work in the community. The rules that Augustine made for monastic life formed the basis of future orders.

In AD 396, Augustine became Bishop of Hippo and never left North Africa again. From this corner of the empire, he set down his beliefs about spiritual redemption, which had a lasting impact on Church teachings.

Augustine lived in a period when the Roman Empire was crumbling under the burden of invading barbarians. Civic order was breaking down. However, Christianity was spreading, albeit haphazardly, across Europe.

Augustine believed the Church to be superior to the state, because its secular duties were based on spiritual qualities. He introduced the doctrine of man's salvation through the grace of God, and his ideas laid the foundations of a Christian political culture.

CATHERINE OF ALEXANDRIA

THIS COURAGEOUS AND INTELLIGENT WOMAN OUT-ARGUED LEARNED PHILOSOPHERS IN DEFENCE OF CHRISTIANITY. SHE WAS TORTURED ON TWO SPIKED WHEELS AND THEN BEHEADED.

KEY FACTS

Virgin martyr
DATES: *4th century AD*
BIRTH PLACE: *Unknown*
PATRON OF: *Philosophers, young female students, librarians, nannies and wheelwrights*
FEAST DAY: *25 November*
EMBLEM: *Jagged wheel and the sword that beheaded her*

The legend of St Catherine of Alexandria is a gorgeous and romantic tale of heroism and faith.

Catherine was the beautiful young daughter of King Costus of Cyprus. She was also clever and courageous. A Christian, she confronted Emperor Maxentius about his persecution of her community.

He was amused and intrigued, and challenged her to a debate with 50 philosophers. On learning that her arguments had converted these learned men, he ordered all 50 to be burnt on a pyre, and had Catherine beaten. Unfortunately for the emperor's wife, she and 200 soldiers were converted too, and also executed.

Isolated in prison, Catherine had doves come to feed her. Then she was "despoiled naked and beaten with scorpions". But no punishments affected her body or her convictions. Maxentius then tried to tempt her with wealth and status, and asked the beautiful Christian to become his wife.

CATHERINE'S DEATH

When Catherine refused he devised a cruel death. She was to be turned between two wheels spiked with blades. But the blades broke and the splinters killed and injured the onlookers. An angel rescued Catherine. No torture could make the girl forsake her faith or her virginity. Even her beheading confounded the emperor. Instead of blood, milk flowed from her virginal veins.

Angels, or perhaps monks, are said to have lifted her body and carried it to Mount Sinai. There it remains, in a monastery built in AD 527 by Emperor Justinian.

Left St Catherine poses, calm and fearless, against her torture wheel (detail from a painting by the studio of Lucas Cranach, 1510).

Catherine had an early cultus in the East, possibly originating near Mount Sinai, and it seems the Crusaders brought her story to the West. Her story is featured in the *Golden Legend*.

Catherine was removed from the Church's Calendar of Saints in 1969, but people continued to venerate her as the bride of Christ (for refusing to marry) and patron of advocates and the dying. A limited recognition of her cultus and sainthood was allowed in 2001.

Above A medieval woman depicted as St Catherine (Dante Gabriel Rossetti, 1857).

URSULA

THIS BEAUTIFUL DAUGHTER OF A CHRISTIAN KING OF ENGLAND IS SAID TO HAVE TURNED DOWN AN OFFER OF MARRIAGE FROM ATTILA THE HUN ON ACCOUNT OF HER FAITHFUL VOW OF VIRGINITY.

KEY FACTS
Virgin martyr
DATES: *4th or 5th century AD*
BIRTH PLACE: *Unknown*
PATRON OF: *Girls, students, the Ursuline Order*
FEAST DAY: *21 October*
EMBLEM: *Crown and huddle of women under her opened cloak*

It is uncertain in which century St Ursula lived, or even that she lived at all. A mound of bones in a burial ground was uncovered in Germany in the 8th century, and in the 10th century an inscription bearing the name Ursula, a 12-year-old girl, was found at the same site. From this "evidence", a medieval legend grew.

Ursula was a British princess during the 4th or 5th century. As a dedicated follower of Christ, she vowed to remain a virgin. She is said to have refused a marriage arranged by the court. In other versions she was betrothed to a pagan and did not refuse him but, instead, set out to convert him.

PILGRIMAGE TO ROME
She requested that, before the wedding, she make a pilgrimage. Either she ran away, or was allowed to board a ship with 11,000 young women, also avowed to Christ and virginity.

This crowd reached Rome where they venerated the saints and their relics. Ursula apparently had a meeting with the pope, one Cyriacus (unknown in papal records). Ursula and her hand-maidens then turned back and sailed the Rhine to Germany.

They stopped in Cologne but invading Huns had taken the city. These barbarians slaughtered the 11,000 Christian women, but not Ursula. The princess was spared because her beauty had been noticed by Attila, warrior leader of the Huns. He desired her, even offering marriage. But her refusal, on account of her vows angered

Above St Ursula Bidding Farewell to her Parents *(the Master of the Legend of St Ursula, before 1482).*

Below St Ursula and her companions are martyred (16th century).

the Hun, whereupon he ordered his archers to shoot her through with arrows.

In Cologne, the romance of Ursula and her maidens was supported by old rumours of an early martyrdom of many young women in the city. The city's basilica was rebuilt to honour them. The story led to a brisk circulation of relics and forged inscriptions. Then, in the 11th century, Elizabeth of Schönau claimed visions of Ursula, and made revelations in her name.

The Roman Catholic Church removed Ursula and her Companions from the Calendar of Saints in 1969.

BENEDICT

St Benedict created a monastic life of simplicity, work and prayer for the religious. His rules rejected the grim hardship imposed by founders of more austere orders.

The best way to appreciate the character of St Benedict is by studying his Rule. These guides to daily living reveal a man who understood the perils of power. He knew that extreme forms of discipline were unkind and could even drive men and women mad.

The system Benedict set up was inspired by his own experiences as a young man. Born into a good family in Umbria in the 5th century AD, he was sent as a student to Rome. However, he disliked the riotous living of the city and wandered off through the

Left Saint Benedict with His Monks at the Refectory *(Il Sodoma, c.1505).*

forested valley between Lazio and Abruzzo. Finding the ruins of Nero's palace beside a lake at Subiaco, he settled in a cave there and spent most of his time in prayer and meditation.

Only one person knew of his whereabouts, a monk named Romanus, who secretly delivered him food. Gradually, knowledge of the hermit became common and his fame spread.

MONASTIC BEGINNINGS
Benedict was persuaded to join a nearby monastery, where he was disturbed by the lax, even dissolute, ways of the monks, and set about reforming them. The monks enjoyed their easy life, and determined to poison the abbot.

Legend tells that when the deadly draught was served to Benedict he made the sign of the cross over the cup. It immediately shattered, and a raven carried the shards away.

He returned to the life of a hermit, but he was not left alone, and soon disciples gathered about him. Benedict founded 12 small monasteries, in each placing

Left St Benedict, *shown wearing the black garb of his monastic order (Pietro Perugino, c.1495–98).*

12 monks, over whom he served as abbot. The houses all gained a reputation for orderly, learned living, without austerity.

RULE OF THE ORDER

Benedict perceived that prayer, routine and purposeful activity were the paths to serenity and to God. Authority was to be controlled. If a monk were to commit a major transgression, the abbot must, before fixing on a punishment, seek the advice of everyone in the monastery, even the youngest.

Though the abbot's decision was final, he must be minded that his decisions would be judged by God. Benedict recommended a simple but ample diet, though no flesh should be served, and the first meal should be around noon.

Benedict allowed for sensible hours of sleep. Property was communal, and the monks had to work, either producing food, maintaining the monastery, or spending time reading and writing the scriptures. But more important than any other duty was regular communal prayer. This he called "divine work".

MONTE CASSINO

Soon Benedict's order became established and noble families sent their sons to his monasteries. These boys were destined to be monks and their training began

SCHOLASTICA

Scholastica, the sister of St Benedict, followed her brother to Monte Cassino. She founded a nunnery about five miles from her brother's monastery. They met once a year, and on one visit Scholastica begged him to stay, for she longed to converse with him. But he refused, so she prayed for rain. It is said that a thunderstorm started and so he stayed the night. Alas, she died three days later, and Benedict then wrote about his conversation with Scholastica during which they discussed their faith.

Above John the Evangelist, Scholastica and Benedict *(the Master of Liesborn, c. 1470-80).*

early. It is said that Benedict saved two of these youths from drowning by walking across water to rescue them.

They became his favourite disciples, Maurus and Placid, and were also venerated as saints. When a powerful, jealous priest complained about the abbot, Benedict left Subiaco, taking with him a few disciples, including Maurus and Placid. He climbed a mountain above the village of Cassino. On a plateau he built Monte Cassino, the monastery that would become the centre of religious life in western Europe and which still operates today.

It was the kindly, humane interpretation of the monastic life that made Benedict so popular. He found a way of allowing the religious to live with an austerity suited to their calling, without risking their health or wellbeing.

Left Benedictine monks walking through the monastery of Monte Cassino, Italy.

DAVID OF WALES

AN AUSTERE PRIEST RENOWNED FOR THE HARSHNESS OF THE MONASTIC REGIME HE ESTABLISHED IN WALES, HE NEVERTHELESS BECAME ONE OF THE BEST-LOVED SAINTS IN HIS COUNTRY.

St David is known as Dewi Sant in Wales, and his name is also sometimes translated as Dafydd. He is also given the title Dewi Dyfyrwr, or David Aquaticus, meaning "David, the Water Drinker". This is attributed to the teetotal regime of his monks who drank neither wine nor beer.

Tradition says David had a grand lineage. His father was thought to be of a princely family named Sant, and his mother, St Non, was also well connected. Possibly born in AD 540, David chose the life of a religious and went to study under the Welsh St Paulinus on a remote, unidentified island. He is said to have found the old hermit blind from weeping for the sins of the world, and restored his sight.

There is another report that David made a pilgrimage to the Holy Land where he was consecrated as an archbishop by the patriarch of Jerusalem.

AUSTERE ORDERS

When David attended the Synod of Victory at Caerleon he was uncompromsing in his stand against the Pelagian movement. This heresy claimed it was possible to find salvation without the help of divine grace. A decisive victory for the established Church outlawed the British movement. David then focused on founding monastic orders.

He settled with his disciples in Mynyw, a remote corner of Wales, and set up the first of many monasteries. David's rule was renowned for its severity. His monks had to live by hard labour and were not even allowed oxen to help them plough the fields.

Their diet was bread, salt and vegetables, and only water could be drunk. Speech was permitted only when absolutely necessary. The monks prayed without break from Friday evening till dawn on Sundays. The monks were described as "more abstemious than Christian".

David was also a powerful preacher. Once, as he was denouncing Pelagianism to a crowd, the earth swelled into a small hill so that more people could see him. He was made head of the Church in Wales by popular acclaim, and died at Mynyw. Leeks and daffodils are worn to mark his feast day.

There are more than 50 place names and dedications to David in South Wales, with further dedications in Devon, Cornwall and Brittany. David's cult was approved by Callistus in 1120, and two pilgrimages to St David's (Mynyw) in Pembrokeshire were said to equal one pilgrimage to Rome, while three were said to equal a pilgrimage to Jerusalem.

Left Detail from a manuscript depicting St David (15th century).

Right Detail from a manuscript depicting St David playing the harp (French School, 11th century).

LEANDER

IN HIS CAPACITY AS BISHOP OF SEVILLE, THE SON OF THE DUKE OF CARTHAGENA BECAME A PROMINENT DEFENDER OF ORTHODOXY IN THE ARIAN DEBATE, AND DREW UP A RULE FOR SPANISH NUNS.

KEY FACTS
Bishop
DATES: C.*AD 550–600*
BIRTH PLACE: *Carthagena*
FEAST DAY: *27 February*
EMBLEM: *Bishop's vestments*

As a member of the Spanish aristocracy, Leander was well disposed to influence those around him. He was a man who carefully selected projects, then applied his energy to completing them successfully.

In about AD 584, he became Bishop of Seville and turned his attention to the unwelcome dominance of the unorthodox Arians in Spain. He used his position to ensure that, at the Council of Toledo, the orthodox concept of the Holy Trinity was officially confirmed. He then concentrated on converting the Arian Visigoths, a strong presence in the Seville region. Patiently, he set about convincing these people of the truth of the Church.

His third concern was for the lives of nuns, for whom he drew up a Rule that proved highly influential. Leander introduced the practice of singing the Nicene Creed at Mass. His younger brother was St Isidore of Seville.

Below The region around Seville today, where Leander was a bishop in the 6th century AD.

JOHN THE ALMSGIVER

WHEN ST JOHN BECAME PATRIARCH OF ALEXANDRIA, HE APPLIED IDEALS OF CHARITY AND JUSTICE TO THE ADMINISTRATION OF THE CITY EARNING HIM THE EPITHET OF ALMSGIVER.

KEY FACTS
Bishop, Patriarch of Alexandria
DATES: C.*AD 560–620*
BIRTH PLACE: *Amathus, Cyprus*
PATRON OF: *Formerly patron of the Knights of Malta but replaced by John the Baptist*
FEAST DAY: *23 January*
EMBLEM: *Bishop's vestments*

Though it is known John was born in Cyprus, it is uncertain where he lived as an adult with his wife and children. At some point he moved to Egypt where, in about AD 610, he became the Bishop and Patriarch of the archdiocese of Alexandria.

John observed that the heretical Monophysites had been busy in the city. They were persuading Christians to accept their view that Jesus had no humanity and was wholly divine.

Instead of confronting the sect, John thought to weaken them through his own example of humble but generous Christian living. His work included establishing a system of welfare reform, and the building of maternity hospitals and homes for the aged and frail. Citizens with legal or financial problems were invited to seek John's advice at twice-weekly meetings. And he organized relief for refugees after the Persians sacked Jerusalem in AD 614.

These efforts at ameliorating hardships and difficulties much endeared him to the people of Alexandria. Many were persuaded to follow his orthodox beliefs. John died soon after retiring to Cyprus in AD 619.

Above Detail from a manuscript depicting St John the Almsgiver (French School, c.550–616).

GREGORY THE GREAT

FACED WITH MILITARY THREATS FROM GERMANIC TRIBES AND UNEASY RELATIONS WITH CONSTANTINOPLE, ST GREGORY DID MUCH TO STRENGTHEN CHRISTENDOM AT A DIFFICULT TIME.

Although Pope Gregory I dreamed of a life of solitude and prayer, he was the obedient son of a wealthy family and so took up a worldly career. Self-assured and clever, he studied law and then, just 30 years of age, was appointed governor of Rome.

A year later, his father died and Gregory found himself one of the richest men in Rome. At last he revealed his true longings by giving up his position and all his wealth. His house became a monastery and he a simple monk.

The Church was reluctant to miss out on such talented leadership. First it made Gregory deacon of Rome, then an ambassador to the Byzantine court in Constantinople. He spoke no Greek and seemed to use this deficiency as a reason for living a monastic life among the monks of the city.

After a few years, in AD 586, he was recalled to Rome. Although he returned as deacon of the city, again he sought the monastic life. But when Pope Pelagius II died four years later, the people of Rome elected Gregory to succeed

him. Rome was in a terrible condition when Gregory became pope. Over the previous century, the state had been conquered, sacked and pillaged many times. The city was dilapidated, without leadership or administration.

AS POPE

When Gregory took office, a plague was raging through the city. One of his first duties was to seek penitence from the citizens in order to end the disease. And so he led a great processional litany through the ruined streets.

Soon after taking office, he wrote to all his clerics, reminding them to treat their flocks with compassion and generosity. He recommended that church money be given to those in dire straits. The granaries of Rome were filled to feed the needy in times of

Right An altarpiece depicting Gregory the Great (Pedro Torres, 16th–17th century).

Below Canterbury Cathedral where Gregory based his English mission (Wenzel Hollar, c.1650).

KEY FACTS
One of the four great Latin Doctors of the Church
DATES: c.AD 540–604
BIRTH PLACE: *Rome*
PATRON OF: *Music, protection against plague*
FEAST DAY: *3 September*
EMBLEM: *Three-tiered papal crown, dove of the Holy Spirit*

"After having confirmed all his actions to his doctrines, the great consul of God went to enjoy eternal triumphs."

EPITAPH ON ST GREGORY'S TOMB

Right A detail of Saints Augustine and Gregory in The Fathers of the Church *(Michael Pacher, 1480).*

food shortage. Jews were allowed to practise their faith and keep their property without fear of being persecuted.

AFFAIRS OF STATE

A greater worry to Gregory was the barbarian foe. From the very outset of his papacy, Gregory had to find energy to deal with the Lombards, a well-organized Germanic group intent on settling in the Roman Empire.

Their presence threatened Christianity. Gregory induced them to remain beyond the border, and arranged an uneasy truce between their leaders and the Byzantine emperor in Constantinople. However, his relationship with the Byzantines was also tense. He resented the grand titles of office assumed by

ANGELS IN SLAVERY

When wandering the streets of Rome one day, Gregory noticed three boys with golden hair and fair skin. They were Anglo-Saxons to be sold in the slave market. On inquiry, he was informed that the youths were "Angels".

Gregory observed, "They are well named, for they have angelic faces and it becomes such to be companions with the angels in heaven. And who is the king of their province?"

"Aella," came the reply.

"Then," announced Pope Gregory, "Alleluia must be sung in Aella's land."

He felt such pity for these little golden creatures that he determined to spread the gospel to their country.

the Patriarch of Constantinople, who he feared wanted to wrest power from the West. Gregory insisted Rome was the centre of the Church and was successful in strengthening papal authority.

MISSION TO ENGLAND

Denied a life of solitude, Gregory found other ways to serve God directly. After once saving some English boys from slavery, Gregory set his mind on converting England. To this end, he dispatched St Augustine and 40 missionaries to Canterbury. Their success among the Anglo-Saxons gave Gregory deep satisfaction.

His writings about the liturgy were of special value, and his text is still used in the Roman Missal. Gregory died in Rome and was buried in St Peter's Cathedral.

Below Saint Gregory the Great is visited by a dove representing the Holy Spirit as he sits writing letters (Carlo Saraceni, c.1620). The dove of the Holy Spirit is one of his emblems.

ISIDORE OF SEVILLE

KNOWN AS THE "SCHOOLMASTER OF THE MIDDLE AGES", ISIDORE OF SEVILLE WAS FAMOUS FOR WRITING A HUGE ENCYCLOPEDIA, WHICH BECAME A STANDARD REFERENCE WORK FOR CENTURIES.

KEY FACTS
Bishop, historian
DATES: c.*AD 560–636*
BIRTH PLACE: *Carthagena*
FEAST DAY: *4 April*
EMBLEM: *Bishop's vestments, books*

The veneration of St Isidore of Seville rests on his scientific and historical research. For the intellectual discipline involved in academic work, he had to thank his brother Leander, who educated him.

Although not a monk, Isidore learnt the monastic habits of deep thinking and discipline of work. When he succeeded his brother as Bishop of Seville in about AD 600, he continued Leander's mission to lead the Visigoths away from the unorthodox views of Arianism. He made the Church run more efficiently and emphasized duty of service and charity. Above all, believing in the importance of education, Isidore recommended that every diocese should have a Church school.

EDUCATIONIST

His writings were to become major texts in the education of generations of theologians, students and researchers. Isidore wrote 86 biographies of biblical figures, and a handbook on morals and theology. He also produced various liturgical analyses.

But his most important work was a massive encyclopedia, called the *Etymologies* (or *Origines*). This opus covered the arts, medicine, law, theology, history, zoology, anthropology, cosmology, agriculture, science and other subjects. Almost 1,000 medieval manucripts

Above Isidore of Seville gives a book to his sister in this Latin manuscript.

of the *Etymologies* are still in existence. Isidore intentionally did not apply any original thinking when he compiled this text. He wished to present all the knowledge then available to the European world and drew on numerous sources.

His other important writings include *On the Wonders of Nature* and *Chronica Majora,* a history from creation to AD 610, though with emphasis on Spanish history. His scholarship was admired across Christendom and medieval intellectuals thought him equal to St Gregory the Great.

Right Scenes from the Life of St Isidore, *from* Le Miroir Historial *by Vincent de Beauvais (French School, 15th century).*

CUTHBERT

A PURPORTED PROPHET AND HEALER, THE POPULAR ANGLO-SAXON ST CUTHBERT PERSUADED HIS CELTIC FLOCK OF THE CORRECTNESS OF FOLLOWING ROMAN CHURCH CUSTOMS.

KEY FACTS
Bishop, missionary
DATES: c.AD 634–87
BIRTH PLACE: *Possibly Jarrow*
PATRON OF: *Formerly of Lindisfarne*
FEAST DAY: *20 March*

After becoming a monk in Melrose in AD 651, Cuthbert spent ten years striving to be a model ascetic. He followed the practice of the time of standing for hours waist-deep in freezing sea water, and walked miles to visit the sick, whom he was said to heal miraculously.

His appointment as abbot put him in a position of influence. His winning manner and frequent local missions laid the groundwork for replacing the ideas of the Celtic Church with those of the Roman Church. The Synod of Whitby endorsed his view.

After a spell at Lindisfarne Abbey, he retired to Inner Farne as a hermit, only to be recalled to become Bishop of Lindisfarne. The gentle monk had a special affinity with the birdlife of the Farne Islands. After he died, his body reputedly stayed incorrupt.

Left King Siegfried visits St Cuthbert and asks him to accept the bishopric of Lindisfarne, from the Latin manuscript of Life and Miracles of St Cuthbert *by the Venerable Bede (English School, 12th century).*

THE VENERABLE BEDE

NO HARDY MISSIONARY OR INSPIRED LEADER, THIS HOMELY MONK SPENT HIS ENTIRE LIFE IN CLOISTERS. YET HE BECAME THE MOST RESPECTED HISTORIAN IN MEDIEVAL WESTERN CHRISTENDOM.

KEY FACTS
Writer, historian
DATES: *AD 673–735*
BIRTH PLACE: *Sunderland, England*
FEAST DAY: *25 May*
EMBLEM: *Monk with pen at a manuscript*

Above Bede is shown here dictating a translation of St John's Gospel into Anglo-Saxon (James Doyle Penrose, 1906).

At the age of seven, Bede was given to a monastery in Jarrow, Northumbria, and stayed there for the rest of his life. From an early age, he loved singing, studying, reading and writing.

He produced numerous texts on many different subjects and the fame of his learning spread far beyond his native county. The best known of his works, *Ecclesiastical History of the English People*, was written in AD 731, and is still in print.

The book was compiled at a time when Christianity was still relatively new to the Anglo-Saxons of Britain, and the faith is presented as a unifying force for the nation. Unusually for his time, Bede took the trouble to differentiate between fact and hearsay in writing history.

An important biography was his *Life and Miracles of St Cuthbert*. His last work was a translation into Old English of the *Gospel of St John*. It is said he dictated the closing sentences of this work from his deathbed.

RUPERT

KNOWN AS THE "APOSTLE OF THE BAVARIANS", ST RUPERT IS CREDITED WITH ESTABLISHING CHRISTIANITY IN LANDS BORDERING THE RIVER DANUBE AND WITH FOUNDING SALZBURG.

KEY FACTS
Missionary, bishop
DATES: *d.c.AD 710*
BIRTH PLACE: *Unknown*
PATRON OF: *Bavaria, Austria, Salzburg*
FEAST DAY: *27 March*
EMBLEM: *Barrel of salt*

Little is known about Rupert's early life, including his birthplace. He may have been a Frank or an Irishman. However, having committed himself to becoming a missionary, Rupert attained high office in the Church, being elected Bishop of Worms in southern Germany.

At the invitation of the Duke of Bavaria, Theodo II, the saint went to Regensburg in Bavaria. There he founded a church near the Wallersee and dedicated it to St Peter. Rupert moved on to Salzburg and gathered disciples around him. For these followers, he founded a monastery at a site

Left St Rupert in a detail from the Altar of St Hildegard of Bingen, Chapel of St Roch (1896).

now known as the Mönchberg, and a convent, the Nonnberg. His sister, Ermentrude, was appointed as abbess to the nuns. He built a house to accommodate clerks and dedicated another church to St Peter. It is possible that Rupert wished to emulate the great apostle in his life of fearless travel, spreading the faith.

MISSION TO THE DANUBE

Having been appointed Bishop of Salzburg, Rupert made that city his headquarters while he travelled extensively through the lands along the River Danube. This region was still a wild part of Europe. The Frankish empire had not yet extended this far east, so Rupert was blazing a trail into hostile barbarian territory.

He must have been a charismatic preacher, for his success as a missionary was immense. He is credited, too, with opening the salt-mining industry at a place which, before his efforts, held only the crumbling ruins of an old Roman town, Juvavum. He renamed the place Salzburg. Because of this activity, paintings often depict St Rupert with a barrel of salt beside him.

Left A statue of St Rupert located outside the Ruprechtskirche, the oldest church in Vienna.

BONIFACE

ONE OF THE GREAT MISSIONARY SAINTS, ST BONIFACE PLAYED A MAJOR ROLE IN ESTABLISHING CHRISTIANITY IN GERMANY WHERE HE IS SAID TO HAVE CONVERTED FOLLOWERS OF NORSE GODS.

KEY FACTS

Missionary martyr, archbishop
DATES: c.*AD 680–754*
BIRTH PLACE: *Possibly Crediton, Devon, England*
PATRON OF: *Germany, brewers, tailors*
FEAST DAY: *5 June*
EMBLEM: *Axe*

Boniface was born in England but he spent many years in Europe where he became known as the "Apostle to the Germans". For the first 40 years of his life he was a monk, mainly at Nursling, near Southampton. Learned and devoted to biblical studies, Boniface was nevertheless no timid scholar.

The Church recognized his qualities of boldness and effective preaching, and sent him on a hazardous mission to lands still in heathen hands. It is said that in AD 718, armed with an axe, Boniface marched into a shrine dedicated to Thor, the Norse god of thunder.

With one mighty swing of the axe, Boniface is said to have felled the oak that was a key cultic object. The amazed onlookers were so impressed with the power of this man's God that tradition says the Germanic tribes converted to his faith en masse.

TIRELESS MISSIONARY

It is much more likely that these conversions happened over a period of time. But Boniface quickly established a reputation among the people of Bavaria, Württemberg, Westphalia and Hesse as "a man who moved with power", in the words of contemporary reports. Pope Gregory II was equally impressed and gave him the bishopric of Mainz.

Right Detail from a manuscript showing Germans being baptized and the martyrdom of St Boniface at Dokkum (AD 975).

Above St Boniface is here shown in proselytizing mode with his axe (Alfred Rethel, 1832).

Boniface summoned more male and female missionaries from his native country.

In about AD 732, the pope made him archbishop. Boniface increasingly handed over the outward missionary work to his English evangelists, while he concentrated on organizing the new Church in West Germany.

Once satisfied that Christianity had taken firm root in Germany, Boniface turned to France. Many sees were vacant or poorly managed. With the help of the Frankish King Pepin, Boniface reformed those dioceses.

He then turned northwards to Frisia, where pagan communities still existed. He was over 70 when he undertook this mission. Travelling with a small band of disciples, he stopped at a place called Dokkum. Here, Boniface and his fellow missionaries were slaughtered by the very people he had hoped to convert.

St Boniface's surviving Latin correspondence reveals a man of courage and determination, who deserves as high a profile in his native England as he enjoys in Germany. The faithful continue to make pilgrimages to his shrine at Fulda, where his remains lie.

CYRIL AND METHODIUS

THESE BROTHERS ARE VENERATED AS APOSTLES OF THE SOUTHERN SLAVS AND FATHERS OF SLAVIC LITERATURE. ST CYRIL GAVE HIS NAME TO THE MODERN SCRIPT CYRILLIC, DEVISED FROM HIS WORK.

KEY FACTS
Translators of Christian texts and apostles to the Slavs
DATES: *Cyril AD 826–69, Methodius c.AD 815–85*
BIRTH PLACE: *Thessalonica, Macedonia*
PATRON OF: *Europe*
FEAST DAY: *14 February (West)*
EMBLEM: *Books, Cyrillic script*

In 1980, Pope John Paul II decided the brothers, Cyril and Methodius, should share the patronage of Europe with St Benedict. Together, these three saints symbolize the religious and political unity of Eastern and Western Europe.

Cyril and Methodius were scholarly men from Thessalonika, Macedonia. Cyril studied in Constantinople where he earned the nickname, "the philosopher".

MISSION TO MORAVIA

His older brother, Methodius, went on a mission to the Khazars of Russia. He then returned to Greece as abbot of a monastery.

At the request of Prince Rostislav of Moravia, both men were sent on a mission to the Slavic province of Moravia (now part of the Czech Republic). The two missionaries were unique in being Greek monks sent off with

Above *This icon from Bulgaria shows Sts Cyril and Methodius in their role as the inventors of the Cyrillic alphabet.*

Below *A fresco depicting Cyril and Methodius meeting Pope Adrian II (Lionello de Nobili, 1886).*

the blessing of the pope in Rome. Until 1054, the Eastern and Western Churches remained in communion with each other.

The brothers not only preached in Slavonic but began translating the Bible and liturgy into the vernacular. Using Greek letters as a model, they invented an alphabet for Slavonic, later named Cyrillic, after Cyril, the younger brother.

But their mission, while finding converts, aroused much political and theological opposition. Their early supporters, Rostislav and Pope Adrian II, had died, and their replacements condemned the use of Slavonic, asserting that no vernacular language was suitable for use in the Church.

METHODIUS ALONE

After Cyril died in Rome in AD 869, Methodius continued the mission alone. But he was persecuted by Bavarian princes and forces within the Church, and imprisoned by German bishops.

After he had spent two years in a damp cell, Pope John VIII had him released and he continued his work in Moravia. He endeavoured to finish translating the Bible into Slavonic but opposition went on, and he died of exhaustion. Cyril and Methodius are admired for their ecumenism – the desire to unite worshippers, East and West.

WENCESLAS

VENERATION OF ST WENCESLAS FOLLOWED HIS RULE AS A GOOD CHRISTIAN DUKE OF BOHEMIA. HE WAS CRUELLY MURDERED FOR HIS FAITH.

Left St Wenceslas is depicted here in armour, bearing a banner of an eagle, oil on panel (Czech School, 16th century).

KEY FACTS
Ruler of Bohemia
DATES: AD 907–35
BIRTH PLACE: *Prague*
PATRON OF: *Brewers, Czech Republic*
FEAST DAY: *28 September*
EMBLEM: *Crown, dagger*

Despite the conversion of much of Bohemia (now part of the Czech Republic), pagan culture persisted and often took a political hue. When Wenceslas' father, the Duke of Bohemia, died, opposition factions mobilized. His grandmother, St Ludmilla, who had educated the boy as a Christian, was murdered and his mother was banished.

However, the people of Bohemia defeated these factions and chose Wenceslas to be their leader. He allied himself with the Christian Henry I (known as Henry the Fowler) of the Holy Roman Empire. Some nobles, including his pagan brother Boleslav, resented the power the clergy of the new court now had.

Boleslav feared his brother's marriage would produce an heir, further strengthening Christian rule and jeopardizing his own chances of power. Following celebrations at the Feast of Sts Cosmas and Damian, Wenceslas died. Boleslav was implicated in the murder but he later repented and had his brother's relics translated to St Vitus's Church, Prague.

The popular hymn "Good King Wenceslas" reflects his reputation for strength and generosity.

ODO OF CLUNY

SO ADMIRED WAS ST ODO FOR HIS LEADERSHIP THAT EVEN THE SECULAR AUTHORITIES TURNED TO HIM FOR GUIDANCE.

Above A view of the 12th-century Benedictine monastery at Cluny in Burgundy, France.

KEY FACTS
Abbot of the Benedictine Monastery of Cluny
DATES: AD 879–942
BIRTH PLACE: *Tours, France*
PATRON OF: *Rain*
FEAST DAY: *18 November*

Reports say Odo had a good sense of fun and was a sympathetic person. Yet he was also a leader who instilled strict monastic observances across France and Italy.

Brought up by the Duke of Aquitaine, he founded the monastery of Cluny. When Odo was made abbot, he introduced the Rule of St Benedict, with its emphasis on vows of chastity, communal poverty and long periods of silent meditation. Cluny rose to become the most important monastery in Europe and Odo was instrumental in it.

He attained papal protection from secular interference for this monastery and others in Western Europe. By the time he retired from the world, Odo's stature was such that Italian politicians often referred to him for help as an impartial mediator in disputes.

STEPHEN OF HUNGARY

ALSO KNOWN AS STEPHEN THE GREAT, THIS NATIONAL HERO IS CONSIDERED THE ARCHITECT OF AN INDEPENDENT CHRISTIAN HUNGARY AND FOUNDER OF A CHURCH WELFARE SYSTEM.

Filled with reforming zeal, King Stephen was inspired by his faith and sympathy for the oppressed. As king, he reduced the power of the nobles and established a semi-feudal, but secure, social system.

If the hallmark of his rule was charity, it was also fundamentalist. Adultery and blasphemy were crimes not to be tolerated, and marriage between Christians and pagans was forbidden. On the other hand, he helped the poor through his church-building programme. By ensuring there was a church in virtually every diocese, tithes demanded from landlords could feed and clothe the underprivileged.

Stephen encouraged missions and finished building the great monastery of St Martin, begun by his father. His last years were spent in dispute over his successor, because his only son had died.

Right The crown of St Stephen, now held at the Magyar Nemzeti Galeria in Budapest (11th century).

EDWARD THE CONFESSOR

ADMIRED FOR HIS DEVOTION TO GOD AND CARE FOR HIS POORER SUBJECTS, EDWARD WAS THE LAST NATIVE KING TO RULE ENGLAND BEFORE THE NORMAN CONQUEST.

The term "Confessor" refers to the fact that Edward lived his life as a devout follower of Christ. It was said that the king and his wife, Edith, were so holy that they did not consummate their marriage.

Edward became King of England in 1042 during a time of great political turbulence. His father-in-law, Earl Godwine, plotted against him while the Danish king threatened to invade England. Edward was generous to the poor. His subjects believed he could "touch for the king's evil", meaning that simply through touch, the king was able to cure scrofula, a kind of tuberculosis.

Another story surrounded a ring which the king supposedly gave to a beggar. Years later, English pilgrims in the Holy Land met an old man who claimed to be John the Apostle and he gave the travellers the king's ring.

Edward started building Westminster Abbey, however he died before it was consecrated. He was canonized in 1161, and since then many sick people have visited his shrine in Westminster Abbey to pray for a cure. The worn steps to the shrine are evidence to the number of pilgrims. The shrine was dismantled during the Reformation that began under Henry VIII and Edward's body was removed. His relics lie behind the high altar in to this day.

Left A sculpture of Edward the Confessor in the church of San Marco, Florence (Pietro Francavilla, 1589).

STANISLAUS OF CRACOW

THE PATRON OF POLAND WAS A BRAVE REFORMER WHO WOULD NOT ALLOW SPECIAL DISPENSATION TO AN UNREPENTANT KING. ST STANISLAUS WAS MARTYRED FOR HIS UNCOMPROMISING STAND.

KEY FACTS
Martyr saint, bishop
DATES: *1010–79*
BIRTH PLACE: *Szczepanow, Poland*
PATRON OF: *Poland, soldiers in battle*
FEAST DAY: *11 April*
EMBLEM: *Bishop's vestments, sword*

Born into a noble Polish family, Stanislaus was well educated, possibly studying in Paris. He was consecrated a bishop in 1072, having made a reputation as a stern reformer of lapses in Christian behaviour.

In the 11th century, Boleslav II was King of Poland and said to be violent and headstrong. Once he abducted a nobleman's wife and imprisoned her in his palace.

Refusing to repent of this demeaning act, the king incurred the wrath of Stanislaus who publicly excommunicated him

Below The Death of St Stanislaus *(Hungarian, 15th century).*

from the Church. King Boleslav II chased his bishop from the church at Cracow and cornered him in the chapel of St Michael.

The knights who hunted down Stanislaus refused to raise their swords against him, so Boleslav committed the murder himself. The king was later deposed and Stanislaus was acknowleged as a martyr saint.

CANUTE

KING CANUTE OF DENMARK WAS DETERMINED TO TURN HIS NATION TO CHRISTIANITY, BUT HE PAID WITH HIS LIFE FOR IMPOSING RELIGIOUS LAWS AND TAXES THAT RILED THE NOBLES.

KEY FACTS
Martyr king
DATES: *d.1086*
BIRTH PLACE: *Denmark*
PATRON OF: *Denmark*
FEAST DAY: *10 July*
EMBLEM: *Crown, dagger, lance, barefoot king with hair in a fillet*

Two passions drove this King of Denmark. He wished to impose the Christian faith on his subjects and he was determined to gain the English throne.

Twice he tried to invade England. Its countrymen, who resented the rule of French invaders brought by William the Conqueror in 1066, sided with the Danish pretender. His first attack on England was a minor raid on York, but for his second campaign, in 1085, he prepared huge numbers of men.

Not all his subjects supported the invasion. Much had been spent on church buildings, and

Left Stained glass depicting King Canute from the west window of Canterbury Cathedral.

new laws empowered priests at the expense of secular nobles. Annoyed by high taxes and heavy-handed religious laws, they sided with Canute's rebellious brother, Olaf. Under siege in the church of St Alban at Odensee, Canute took the sacrament. As he knelt before the altar, he and 18 followers were stabbed to death.

MARGARET OF SCOTLAND

AN ANGLO-SAXON ROYAL WHO MARRIED A SCOTTISH KING DID MUCH TO REVIVE THE FLAGGING CHURCH IN HIS COUNTRY.

KEY FACTS
Queen
DATES: *1046–93*
BIRTH PLACE: *Hungary*
PATRON OF: *Scotland*
FEAST DAY: *16 November*
EMBLEM: *Crown*

Left A portrait of Margaret published in the Memoirs of the Court of Queen Elizabeth *(c. 1825).*

This cultivated granddaughter of the English king Edmund Ironside was one of the last members of Anglo-Saxon royalty before the Norman Conquest. Indeed, at the invasion she fled northwards and took refuge at the court of Malcolm III of Scotland.

The king was beguiled by her charm and intelligence, and they married in 1069. Her Christian devotion inspired her to revive the Church in Scotland, which had declined since the Celtic heyday of St Columba of Iona and St Aidan. She reformed the abbey at Iona and encouraged pilgrimages and the building of monasteries.

Margaret built Dunfermline church to be a burial place for the Scottish royal family. Her adoring husband, who was at first rough and illiterate, grew to be proud of her generosity toward his subjects, and became as devout a Christian as she was.

Two of her sons became kings of Scotland. She died shortly after hearing of the death of her husband and son in battle.

BENNO OF MUNICH

TORN BETWEEN LOYALTIES, ST BENNO HAD TO SEARCH HIS CONSCIENCE TO MAKE THE RIGHT DECISIONS. HE WAS IMPRISONED AND CASTIGATED, BUT IN ALL HE STROVE ONLY TO SERVE HIS FLOCK.

KEY FACTS
Bishop
DATES: *d. 1107*
BIRTH PLACE: *Saxony*
PATRON OF: *Munich*
FEAST DAY: *16 June*
EMBLEM: *Fish and key*

Born to a noble Saxon family at a time of political strife, Benno was frequently caught up in the agitation. Having been appointed Bishop of Meissen by the German Emperor Henry IV, Benno found himself torn between allegiances. He opted to support his fellow Saxons in their uprising against the emperor.

Henry IV promptly had Benno imprisoned, but then released him on oath of fidelity. However, he reneged on this promise, siding again with the emperor's enemies.

When, as a punishment, his bishopric was removed, Benno vowed allegiance to the anti-pope Guibert in the hope that he might

recover his position as bishop and return to his flock. When this move failed, Benno revived his loyalty to Pope Urban II.

A legend says that when the emperor was excommunicated, Benno decided the best way to stop him entering his cathedral was to throw the key into the river. Benno later found his key miraculously stored inside a fish. The saint's relics were later moved to Munich for safekeeping.

Left The Martyrdom of St Benno (Carlo Saraceni, 1618). Benno was venerated throughout Saxony.

ANSELM

DESPITE FALLING OUT WITH TWO KINGS OF ENGLAND, THE ITALIAN MONK WHO BECAME ARCHBISHOP OF CANTERBURY WAS WIDELY ADMIRED FOR HIS LEARNING AND "PROOF" OF GOD'S EXISTENCE.

KEY FACTS
Doctor of the Church
DATES: *1033–1109*
BIRTH PLACE: *Aosta, Italy*
FEAST DAY: *21 April*
EMBLEM: *A ship, symbolizing spiritual independence*

As a boy, Anselm longed to be a monk. After his mother died when he was 20, Anselm left home to wander as a lone ascetic. He passed through Burgundy and found himself in Normandy, where he was inspired by the teaching of the abbot Lanfranc.

He stayed at Lanfranc's monastery of Bec and in time became its abbot. It was a wealthy establishment. Once Anselm was obliged to visit England to oversee property owned by Bec, and it was on this trip that the Italian monk first met the king.

IN AND OUT OF FAVOUR

He so impressed King William II (Rufus) that, in 1093, he made Anselm archbishop of Canterbury. Though preferring to stay in Bec, Anselm nevertheless accepted the office.

The Italian's reluctance was soon justified when William declared his hand and demanded that he, the king, should appoint all English bishops and abbots henceforth. Anselm claimed that such power resides solely within the Church, and went to Rome to discuss the problem.

In his absence, the king took his opportunity and seized the church revenues. Anselm condemned the action as theft and abandoned Canterbury to live as an exile in Europe.

In 1100, the new English king, Henry I, summoned Anselm back. Again monk and monarch disagreed over appointments, and again Anselm went into exile. By 1107, they finally reached a

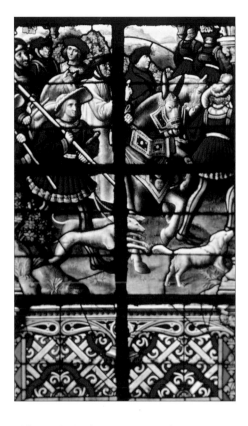

Above A 15th-century window in Tournai Cathedral, Belgium, shows Anselm travelling to consult the pope.

compromise and Anselm returned to office to live out his last years in relative peace.

Exile had provided him with a chance to put down his ideas in writing. Unlike his predecessors, Anselm defended his faith by reason, rather than using scripture as his authority.

Anselm is famous for his "ontological argument" for the existence of God, in which he asserts that the mere idea that there is a God necessarily proves his existence.

Anselm's cult grew slowly, but was helped by a well-written and sympathetic biography of his life written by his friend and disciple, Eadmer of Canterbury. In 1734, in recognition of his position as the most influential Christian writer in the period between Augustine of Hippo and Thomas Aquinas, Anselm was named a Doctor of the Church. He is admired to this day for his steadfastness and piety, and is remembered as an intellectual and philosophical man.

Below Scenes from the Life of St Anselm of Canterbury, *from* Le Miroir Historial by Vincent de Beauvais (French School, 15th century).

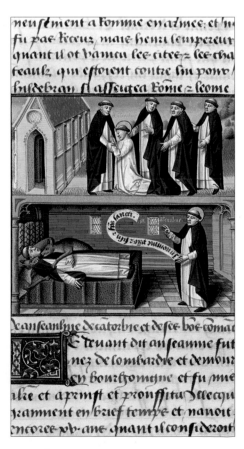

STEPHEN HARDING

ESTABLISHING THE MONASTIC SYSTEM OF THE CISTERCIANS WAS ST HARDING'S GREAT ACHIEVEMENT. HIS IDEAS SPREAD ACROSS WESTERN EUROPE AND REFORMED NEARLY 700 MONASTERIES.

KEY FACTS
Founder of Cistercian monastic order
DATES: *d.1134*
BIRTH PLACE: *England*
FEAST DAY: *28 March*
EMBLEM: *Cistercian habit*

Having settled in France, Stephen Harding, who was English by birth, made a huge impact on the religious history of Europe by helping to found the great monastery of Citeaux. Under his 25-year leadership, this first of the Cistercian monasteries became a model for the austere religious life.

In a bid to return to a strict observance of the Benedictine Rule, Stephen demanded wholesale changes to the dissolute lifestyle of contemporary monks. Luxuries were banned. The monks could no longer enjoy the monastic income derived from their mills, serfs and tithes. They now had to farm the fields themselves and live on their produce alone. Many new monasteries were built in remote places to avoid contact with town folk.

Stephen expected each abbot to visit the monasteries under his care and report to Citeaux. Thus he maintained his high standards.

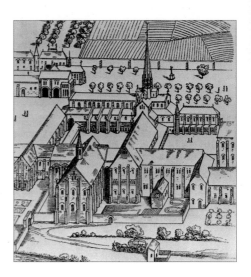

Right A woodcut of the Cistercian monastery at Citeaux, France, founded in 1098.

NORBERT

NORBERT GAVE UP A WEALTHY LIFE TO BECOME A MONASTIC REFORMER. HE SET UP THE SO-CALLED "WHITE CANONS", WHICH SPREAD QUICKLY OVER WESTERN EUROPE, ESPECIALLY HUNGARY.

KEY FACTS
Founder of order, archbishop
DATES: *c.1080–1134*
BIRTH PLACE: *Xanten, Prussia*
FEAST DAY: *6 June*
EMBLEM: *Bishop's vestments*

Like St Francis of Assisi, Norbert was born into a wealthy family and then abandoned his worldly privileges. Norbert almost died in a thunderstorm in 1115. This experience inspired him to give away his possessions and beg the pope for forgiveness for his past life. To atone for his sins, he became a wandering preacher in northern France and the Low Countries.

Norbert's sternness of faith and eschewing of worldly things did not endear him to all the clergy. To put his beliefs into practice, he founded a community in Prémontré in the Rhineland,

where he instituted an austere regime following the rules of St Augustine of Hippo. Norbert was a friend of St Bernard of Clairvaux and shared his reforming zeal.

Although there were clergy who resented his ideas, Norbert was generally popular. In 1126, he was appointed Archbishop of Magdeburg. His monastic order, known as the Premonstratensians, or "White Canons", after their vestments, gained ground quickly.

Left A portrait of St Norbert from an illuminated manuscript (11th–12th century).

BERNARD OF CLAIRVAUX

UNDER THE LEADERSHIP OF ST BERNARD, THE CISTERCIAN ORDER GREATLY INFLUENCED THE SPIRITUAL DIRECTION CHRISTIANITY WOULD TAKE DURING MEDIEVAL TIMES.

KEY FACTS

Doctor of the Church
DATES: *c. 1090–1153*
BIRTH PLACE: *Fontaines, near Dijon, France*
PATRON OF: *Gibraltar*
FEAST DAY: *20 August*
EMBLEM: *Beehive, beekeepers, candle-makers, Eucharistic host*

St Bernard was one of the most charismatic figures of the medieval Church. His powerful preaching, energy and dedication to leading a model Christian life made him an influential force in the Church, though not one that always met with approval.

Fervent in his commitment to reforming monastic life, Bernard followed the example set by Stephen Harding, and joined his monastery at Citeaux. His clarity of vision for the developing Cistercian Order naturally led to Bernard's appointment in 1115 as abbot of the poverty-stricken Clairvaux, the third Cistercian monastery.

Critical of the gentler, parallel order at Cluny, known as the "Black Benedictines", Bernard was determined to establish an austere discipline without compromise, surviving on minimal rations and hard labour.

Starting with just 30 fellow devotees, his way blossomed despite its rigours. It is said that his charm and facility to heal the sick attracted thousands of pilgrims. By his death, the number of monks at Clairvaux alone had risen to 700, while some 400 Cistercian monasteries were established across Europe.

POLITICS AND CRUSADE

Bernard's enthusiasm, coupled with his eloquence, inevitably drew him into church politics. At this time, the authority of the Roman Church was jeopardized by disputes over who should be pope. The princes of Europe tended to back one candidate or another. Bernard's successful promotion of Eugenius III to the papacy in 1145 did much to raise his public profile. Soon he was being asked to combat the rising Albigensian heresy in southern France, which he condemned with characteristic fervour.

Perhaps Bernard's greatest challenge was promoting the Second Crusade (1145–49) to recover the Holy Land from Muslim control. His stirring speeches inspired thousands of the good, the bad, even criminals, to "take the Cross". To protect Christians travelling to Palestine, Bernard took control of the Cistercian Order of Knights Templar and devised a chivalric code of conduct. Following the failure of the crusade, Bernard's esteem suffered a great deal, allowing his enemies to make capital out of the disaster.

Bernard's eloquent articulation of his faith is nowhere more evident than in his surviving letters and sermons, and in his treatise on the Love of God.

Below St Bernard of Clairvaux *(Ferrer Bassa, 14th century).*

HENRY OF FINLAND

AN ENGLISH BISHOP OF UPPSALA, SWEDEN, HENRY JOINED A CRUSADE TO FINLAND IN ORDER TO CONVERT ITS WAR-LIKE PEOPLE, AND REMAINED THERE AS A MISSIONARY.

KEY FACTS
Martyr bishop
DATES: *d.1156*
BIRTH PLACE: *England*
PATRON OF: *Finland,
sea fishermen*
FEAST DAY: *20 January*
EMBLEM: *Bishop's vestments*

Henry was a soldier for Christ. In 1154, he joined King Eric IX of Sweden's war against the Finns. The king saw his military expedition as a crusade and offered the Finns peace if they became Christian. They refused and were defeated in battle.

Henry stayed in Finland and he baptized many of the people. He built a church at Nousis, which became the centre of his missionary work. Eventually, he was killed

by a Finnish convert when he refused to grant him forgiveness for killing a Swedish soldier. His cultus spread and he became Finland's patron saint.

Left St Henry of Finland from the Sforza Hours, *one of the most beautiful Renaissance manuscripts extant (Giampietrino Birago, c.1490).*

ERIC OF SWEDEN

ERIC HOPED TO INTRODUCE CHRISTIAN RULE TO HIS COUNTRYMEN BUT WAS MURDERED IN DENMARK WHEN HE TRIED TO USE HIS MILITARY MIGHT TO SPREAD HIS CHRISTIAN MESSAGE.

KEY FACTS
Martyr king
DATES: *d.1160*
BIRTH PLACE: *Sweden*
PATRON OF: *Sweden*
FEAST DAY: *18 May*
EMBLEM: *Crown*

Through his marriage to Christine, of the Swedish royal family, Eric was able to claim the throne in 1156. Committed to his faith, he instituted a Christian legal system and channelled funds into the Church.

However, disgruntled Swedes opposed to his reforms sought allies abroad to back a rebellion. In 1154, one such ally arose in Denmark. Determined to spread Christianity across Scandinavia, Eric waged war against any neighbouring peoples who would not accept Christianity as their faith. He began by invading Finland. When he continued into Denmark, he was outnumbered by a united force of Danes and rebel Swedes. As Eric left Mass on Ascension Day, he was cut down by Danish soldiers. Lying humiliated at their feet, he was subjected to terrible torture and beheaded.

A cultus quickly developed around Eric. Ironically, Nordic mythology possibly played its part in raising his profile to that of national hero, residing in the heavenly abode of Valhalla.

Eric's body and kingly regalia were laid in a new cathedral built in Uppsala, and he was adopted as patron of Sweden. Until the Reformation, farmers would hold annual processions begging Eric's intercession for good harvests.

Left The coronation of Eric of Sweden (Italian School, 19th century).

THOMAS BECKET

THE TRAGIC MURDER IN CANTERBURY CATHEDRAL OF THIS DEVOUT PRIEST CREATED SUCH A SENSATION THAT PILGRIMS CAME FROM ALL OVER MEDIEVAL CHRISTENDOM TO VISIT HIS SHRINE.

KEY FACTS
Martyr, archbishop
DATES: *1118–70*
BIRTH PLACE: *London*
PATRON OF: *Clergy*
FEAST DAY: *29 December*
EMBLEM: *Tonsured (crown of head shaved), holding archbishop's cross, mitre*

The clever son of a wealthy family, Thomas was a man of the world in his early career as archdeacon of Canterbury. He was just the sort of pleasure-loving priest that appealed to the young King of England, Henry II.

The king soon appointed him Chancellor of England. In this capacity, Thomas entertained lavishly and travelled abroad on diplomatic missions on behalf of his friend, the king.

ARCHBISHOP

Henry ensured Thomas was made Archbishop of Canterbury in 1162 but, to his intense annoyance, Thomas repented of his former ways. Instead, he became a dutiful, austere religious, wearing a hairshirt and holding long prayer vigils.

No longer the carefree friend, Thomas began to upbraid the king on matters of taxation, reminding him of the Church's rights and privileges. Henry was further enraged when Thomas insisted God and Rome were the supreme authorities, not the King of England. Henry wished to try the clergy in the courts of England, but Thomas claimed this was unacceptable, that they had the right to appeal to Rome.

EXILE AND MURDER

The differences between the two men descended into bitter squabbles, including disputes over money. Thomas went into exile, seeking refuge in a Cistercian monastery in France. After six

Above Detail from a medieval manuscript showing the murder of Thomas Becket (English School).

years, he believed reconciliation had been reached, and returned to Canterbury in hope.

To his great dismay, he discovered his land had been appropriated and his followers alienated. But Thomas continued to assert his allegiance to God over the state. Henry, demanding and quick-tempered, was exasperated. In an outburst, his uttered wish to be rid of "this turbulent priest" was taken at face value by four nearby barons.

His henchmen sped off to the cathedral in Canterbury and, after a brief altercation with Thomas, set upon him with their swords. The king did public penance for this savage murder, but the veneration of Thomas as a martyr spread fast. Hundreds of miracles were claimed in his name and his shrine became one of the most popular in all Christendom.

Below Henry II of England arguing with Thomas Becket (English School, 14th century).

FRANCIS OF ASSISI

THROUGHOUT THE WORLD TODAY, FRANCISCAN MONKS AND NUNS CONTINUE THE CHARITY WORK BEGUN BY THEIR FOUNDER, WHOSE PURE LOVE OF CREATION INSPIRED A NEW ATTITUDE TO THE WORLD.

Few saints are held in such high esteem for their spirit of devotion as is St Francis. The humble friar wished for nothing other than to imitate Christ. For him the world was an expression of God, and this conviction gave him a special affinity with nature.

REJECTING WEALTH

Francis was born into a rich Italian family and as a youth enjoyed his privileged status. But in the course of a war between Assisi and Perugia, he was imprisoned and began to question his spiritual life. After the war he

KEY FACTS
First saint to receive the stigmata, in 1224
DATES: *1181–1226*
BIRTH PLACE: *Assisi, Italy*
PATRON OF: *Animals and birds, ecologists, merchants*
FEAST DAY: *4 October*

Left Scenes from the life of St Francis of Assisi *(Bonaventura Berlinghieri, 1235). This panel is the earliest known depiction of this saint.*

started to give away money to the poor and once, so overcome with compassion, he kissed the diseased hand of a leper.

His father was so angry at this bizarre behaviour that he demanded his son renounce his inheritance. In fact, Francis was glad to do so, for he had heard a voice telling him to live without property, and to preach the word of God. Francis left his family to take up a life of poverty.

NEW ORDER

Francis lived near the ruined chapel of St Mary of the Angels, known as the Portiuncula, near Assisi. He took shelter in a bare hut, and cared for the local lepers.

His preaching and devotion attracted followers, impressed by the simplicity and humility of Francis's faith. In 1210, Pope Innocent III authorized Francis and 11 companions to be "roving preachers of God".

Franciscans travelled in pairs preaching his philosophy of poverty and living by begging. The order soon spread across Europe as far as England.

Left The Lower Church of San Francesco in Assisi, Italy, built in the 13th century.

Mountains where he fasted for 40 days with his followers. While there he had a vision of an angel who enveloped him with light.

Francis then famously received the stigmata. His hands, feet and side are said to have manifested the same wounds that Christ received at the Crucifixion. The marks stayed with him for the rest of his life. In 1226, blind yet filled with joyous faith, Francis died at Portiuncula.

> "Most high, all-powerful, all good, Lord!
> All praise is yours, all glory, all honour
> And all blessing.
>
> To you alone, Most High, do they belong.
> No mortal lips are worthy
> To pronounce your name.
>
> All praise be yours, my Lord, through all that you have made,
> And first my lord Brother Sun,
> Who brings the day; and light you give to us through him.
>
> How beautiful is he, how radiant in all his splendour!
> Of you, Most High, he bears the likeness."

THE FIRST FOUR VERSES OF THE CANTICLE OF BROTHER SUN

Despite poor health, Francis made several journeys to convert Muslims living around the Mediterranean Sea. Once, when he was taken prisoner during a battle in Egypt between Crusaders and Muslims, the local sultan was so touched by his

Above St Francis Prays to the Birds, *fresco from the church of San Francesco in Assisi (c.1260).*

devotion and disdain of wealth that he was released. In 1219, he reached the Holy Land, but the following year the Franciscans recalled him to Europe.

SPIRITUAL RETREAT
The order had grown hugely in his absence and Francis handed control to the able administrator, Elias of Cortona. It was he who now maintained the Franciscan Rule, which insisted on possessing no money or property, teaching the word of Christ, and caring for the sick and needy. In 1224, Francis retreated to the Apennine

> "Lord grant me the serenity to accept the things I cannot change, the courage to change the things I can, and the wisdom to know the difference."
>
> ST FRANCIS OF ASSISI

THOMAS AQUINAS

THE "ANGELIC DOCTOR" WAS AN INTELLECTUAL GIANT OF THE MEDIEVAL CHURCH WHO EXPANDED CHRISTIAN THINKING TO ESTABLISH A COMPREHENSIVE DOCTRINE OF THE CATHOLIC FAITH.

This well-built man was dubbed the "dumb ox" for his gentle courtesy and because he was thought to be a little slow of mind. But as his energy and output was to demonstrate, Thomas Aquinas outstripped all his contemporaries in intellectual capacity.

One writer said that the amount of study required to produce all Aquinas' books would take several normal lifetimes. However, his aristocratic family did not share the young man's enthusiasm to join the Dominicans, a mendicant order that lived by begging.

HOUSE ARREST

His family, who regarded the mendicants' activities as shameful, had educated Thomas at the reputable Benedictine monastery at Monte Cassino, whose abbot was related to the Aquino family. When the determined prodigy nevertheless joined the Black Friars at the age of 21, his brothers kidnapped him and imprisoned him at the family home.

But Thomas would not relent. His family even sent a beautiful girl to tempt him from his chosen path. Paintings depict him brandishing a burning stick to ward away the temptress.

FAITH AND REASON

Eventually released, Thomas went to Cologne, Germany, to study under St Albert the Great. This teacher provided the groundwork for much of Aquinas' theology. Thenceforth, he was to spend his

Left Temptation of St Thomas Aquinas *(Diego Rodríguez de Silva y Velásquez, 17th century).*

KEY FACTS

Theologian and writer
DATES: *c.1225–74*
BIRTH PLACE: *Rocca Secca, near Aquino, Italy*
PATRON OF: *Academics, universities, schools, students, theologians, pencil-makers*
FEAST DAY: *28 January*
EMBLEM: *Star shedding light, ox, books, lily*

"We should show honour to the saints of God, as being members of Christ, the children and friends of God, and our intercessors. Therefore, in memory of them we ought to honour any relics of theirs in a fitting manner."

ST THOMAS AQUINAS

life moving back and forth between France and Italy as a teacher and academic.

In tandem with St Albert the Great, Thomas Aquinas believed in the harmony of faith and reason. Hitherto, theological points of debate had taken the Bible as their authority. Now Aquinas was asserting that reasoned argument was authority in itself because God gave mankind the power of reason.

ARISTOTLE AND ISLAM

Aquinas held that everything comes from God. He said that at the end of their lives humans return to God as to their home.

A perfect life was one that combined contemplation with action, since it is only through prayer that we can know the will of God. At the time that Aquinas

Below St Thomas Aquinas *(Abraham Jansz Diepenbeeck, c.1640–50).*

Left St Thomas Aquinas wearing Dominican garb and praying at the altar, from Libro de Horas de Alfonso el Magnifico, *the vellum prayer book of Alfonso V of Aragon (Spanish School, c.1442).*

lived, Islamic scholars were bringing ideas of the ancient Greek philosophers, such as Aristotle, back to Europe. In debate with Muslims, Aquinas produced an entire book responding to their writings.

His intellect aimed not only at the higher reaches of the Church. Some of the most beautiful hymns written for Mass have been ascribed to him and he produced prayers and expositions of the Creed for the ordinary believer. He was also a preacher, giving sermons on the Ten Commandments and key tenets of the Christian faith.

SPIRITUAL END

In about 1266, Aquinas began his *Summa Theologica,* a study of all the Christian mysteries, which ran to five volumes. He never finished the work because in 1272 he had a profound mystical experience while attending Mass.

The effect of receiving a vision of God, as he reported, was so overwhelming that he felt his intellect no longer adequate. Indeed, he is famously reputed to have said that all he had written to date was "like straw" compared to this spiritual experience.

Not long after this event, he prepared to attend the Council at Lyons but was taken ill on the journey. He died at the abbey of Fossanuova aged 43.

SUMMA THEOLOGICA

Having produced a text, *Summa contra Gentes,* that presented the faith to non-believers, Thomas Aquinas set about writing his *magnum opus* to instruct beginners in Roman Catholic theology. Running to five volumes, *Summa Theologica* covers a great variety of subjects.

The first volume explains all that emanates from God. The second volume explains the psychology of human activity and its organization. The third asserts that humans return to God as to their natural home. The fourth volume discusses the Holy Spirit, and a life of meditation and action. And the fifth, unfinished, summarizes faith.

Above Title page from Summa Theologica *on vellum (French School, 14th century).*

THERESA OF ÁVILA

THIS DEVOUT NUN COURTED CONTROVERSY DURING HER LIFETIME BY CHALLENGING THE ESTABLISHED CARMELITE ORDER AND BY CLAIMING NUMEROUS VISIONS AND COMMUNICATIONS WITH CHRIST.

KEY FACTS
Mystic, virgin
DATES: *1515–82*
BIRTH PLACE: *Avila, Spain*
PATRON OF: *Spain, Spanish Catholic writers, Carmelites*
FEAST DAY: *15 October*
EMBLEM: *Pen and book, an angel, burning lance or arrow*

Theresa de Capeda y Ahumada was born at Ávila to a wealthy Castilian family. She was a bright, independent girl whose piety was evident from an early age. After her mother's death, her father sent her to an Augustinian convent, where she discovered her calling to the Church. Aged 20, and against her father's wishes, she entered a Carmelite convent. Within a short time, however, Theresa was taken gravely ill and left the convent to be cared for by her family. Although she never regained full health, she returned to the Carmelites where she enjoyed the sociable, relaxed environment of the Order.

Following the death of her father in 1543, Theresa became committed to a more private,

Below Theresa of Ávila's Vision of a Dove *(Peter Paul Rubens, c.1614).*

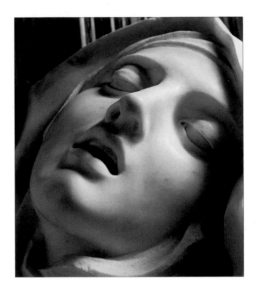

Above Detail of the Ecstasy of Saint Theresa, *held in the Church of Santa Maria della Vittoria in Rome (Gianlorenzo Bernini, c.1645–52).*

contemplative life. One particular incident changed her life: she collapsed in front of an image of Christ, later waking and realizing she must renounce all worldly emotion and live only for Him.

VISIONARY

From the moment of her conversion, Theresa had visions and went into deep spiritual trances when she prayed. She felt misunderstood by her fellow nuns who were dismissive of her mystic experiences. For the rest of her life she continued to have rapturous visions. In particular, she suffered a pain in her side, inflicted, she claimed, by an angel who thrust a burning lance into her heart. Her powers of contemplation developed into a deep devotion and she referred to herself as "Theresa of Jesus".

REFORMER

After meeting Peter of Alcantara, Theresa was moved to follow his example of strict penance and mental prayer. She requested permission from the pope to open a small house. The order would be named St Joseph after her patron saint. When the secret plans were revealed, the Carmelite nuns and influential people of Ávila asked the pope to stop them. Theresa appealed to Spain's King Philip II, who resented Rome's authority. This caused angry confrontation between Church and state and Theresa was imprisoned for two

"St Theresa, grant that my every thought, desire and affection may be continually directed to doing the will of God, whether I am in joy or in pain, for He is worthy to be loved and obeyed forever. Obtain for me this grace, thou who art so powerful with God; may I be all on fire, like thee, with the holy love of God."

PRAYER OF INTERCESSION TO ST THERESA OF ÁVILA

years before she was permitted to open a Carmelite sub-group. Her nuns, known as Discalced, or Barefoots, wore coarse brown habits and rope sandals to show their lives of poverty.

During the next few years, Theresa travelled across Spain establishing convents. Her nuns were separated from the world, lived on alms, were forbidden to eat meat, and were instructed by Theresa in meditation.

She founded 16 convents and 14 monasteries, because men, too, wanted to take the vows of the Discalced. These male orders were organized with the help of another mystic, John of the Cross.

Below The Communion of St Theresa of Ávila (*Claudio Coello, 17th century*).

Left Saint Theresa of Ávila (*Gregorio Fernandez, 1625*).

Theresa's writings are testament to her great personal devotion and her thoughts on a life of prayer and contemplation. Chief among her works are *The Interior Castle* and *The Way of Perfection*. The books, which describe the journey of the "soul toward a perfect unity with God", continue to be published in numerous languages.

Theresa of Ávila died at the convent of Alba de Tormes. The odour of violets and sweet oil emanated from her tomb. It was opened and a hand was cut off illicitly, and this was found to work miracles. Her remains were reburied in 1585 in a tomb built by the Duke of Alba. Theresa was canonized by Pope Gregory XV in 1622, and declared a Doctor of the Church in 1970, the first woman to win this recognition. Her order continues to prove the need for retreat and prayer in the modern world.

ST PETER OF ALCANTARA

St Theresa of Ávila was inspired by the life and teachings of another great mystic, Peter of Alcantara. Born Peter Garavito, he was ordained a Franciscan, but longed for a more rigorous discipline. In 1538, he became head of the strict order in Estremadura, Spain, but met with opposition when he tried to reform them further. He went on to found a small, reformed Alcantrine Franciscan order at a friary in Pedrosa. Peter encouraged Theresa to follow his rules of avoiding meat and wine, and walking barefoot. His treatise on prayer and meditation has been translated into many languages. He was canonized in 1669.

Above St Peter of Alcantara visited by a dove (engraving by A. Masson after a painting by Francisco de Zurbarán, c. 1560).

ROBERT BELLARMINE

AMONG HIS MANY ACHIEVEMENTS, THE BRILLIANT THEOLOGIAN ROBERT BELLARMINE WAS RESPONSIBLE FOR CORRECTING THE VULGATE BIBLE AND WRITING A CATECHISM, BOTH IN USE TODAY.

KEY FACTS
Archbishop and theologian
DATES: *1542–1621*
BIRTH PLACE: *Montepulciano, Tuscany, Italy*
PATRON OF: *Catechists and catechumens*
FEAST DAY: *17 September*
EMBLEM: *Archbishop's vestments*

This great Italian archbishop chose a life of service to God over a secular career. Despite his father's wishes that he become a politician, Robert Bellarmine entered a novitiate in Rome and went on to teach in Jesuit colleges in Rome and Florence.

GIFTED THEOLOGIAN

After his ordination in 1570, Robert became the first Jesuit professor of the University of Louvain. It was here that his writings and lectures began to stir strong feelings and debate. The Church brought him to Milan as professor of controversial theology at the Roman College. The lectures he gave there formed the basis of one of his greatest works, *Disputations on the Controversies of the Christian Faith*, which is described as "the most complete defence of Catholic teaching yet published". It was read eagerly by all Christians, although his enemies

Above St Robert Bellarmine, in a painting from the church of Sant-Ignazio in Rome.

Below The trial of Galileo by Pope Urban VIII during the Inquisition in 1633 (Italian School, 17th century).

denounced it as being so clever it must have been the joint effort of several Jesuit scholars. The work was banned in England.

CONTROVERSY

Robert continued to attract controversy when his stand on the power of the Church was opposed by the French and by James I of England because he insisted the pope had complete authority above that of any monarch. His *De potestate papae* on this subject was burnt by the Paris parlement. Then, contrary to other Church leaders at the time, Robert was gentle with Galileo, asking him only to produce better evidence about the sun's movements.

Appointed Archbishop of Capua in 1602, Robert dedicated his time to preaching and to attending to his parish. His last appointment, in 1605, was as Prefect of the Vatican Library.

SIMPLE LIFE, NOBLE DEATH

All his life, Robert Bellarmine lived on the bread and garlic diet of a peasant, denied himself fires in winter and gave his possessions to the poor. In old age, he continued to write, and his *Art of Dying* was translated into many languages. He died in Rome, but he had asked beforehand that the day of his death be marked each anniversary as a time to honour the Stigmata of St Francis of Assissi. The Church granted this request.

FRANCIS OF SALES

THE FIRST SOLEMN BEATIFICATION TO TAKE PLACE IN ST PETER'S IN ROME WAS THAT OF ST FRANCIS OF SALES, A SAINT WHO WAS ADORED FOR HIS GENTLE LEADERSHIP.

KEY FACTS

Founder, Doctor of the Church
DATES: *1567–1622*
BIRTH PLACE: *Château de Sales,*
Savoy, France
PATRON OF: *Journalists, editors*
and writers
FEAST DAY: *24 January*
EMBLEM: *Archbishop's vestments*

Francis of Sales was physically frail from birth, but had a determined spirit and an unwavering faith. From an early age, he longed to join the Church. But his father refused his permission, instead sending Francis to study at the University of Paris. He later became a Doctor of Law at Padua in Italy. When a relative found Francis a position as provost to the Jesuit chapter in Geneva, his father finally relented and Francis was ordained.

Left St Francis de Sales in the Desert *(Marco Antonio Franceschini, c.1700–10).*

privileges for his community. In every village he passed, people wanted him to stop and minister to them. It was bitterly cold, but Francis continued to preach throughout Advent and Christmas, before becoming ill and dying at a Visitandine convent in Lyons.

MISSIONARY PRIEST

Francis volunteered as a missionary to Chablais, where he distributed notices explaining his work and Christ's message to attract his reluctant congregation. Trekking through isolated hamlets, he met many dangers, including an attack by a wolf and another by an angry mob. Yet, slowly, lapsed Catholics began to seek his guidance.

His success was acknowledged, and in 1602, the Church appointed him Bishop of Geneva. Francis lived in Annecy, where he was a popular preacher and began to compile his handwritten texts into books. His most famous work is the *Introduction to the Devout Life*. In addition to his writing, Francis was instrumental in the founding of the Order of the Visitation with his friend, St Jane Frances de Chantal in 1610.

In 1622, Francis accepted an invitation to join the Duke of Savoy at Avignon, hoping to gain

Right St Francis of Sales *(Noel Halle, 18th century).*

PETER CLAVER

THIS SPANISH MISSIONARY WAS BLESSED "BY GOD WITH THOSE GIFTS THAT PARTICULARLY PERTAIN TO APOSTLES, OF MIRACLES, OF PROPHECY AND OF READING HEARTS".

KEY FACTS
Missionary
DATES: *1580–1654*
BIRTH PLACE: *Verdu, Catalonia, Spain*
PATRON OF: *Colombia; missions to slaves and African Americans*
FEAST DAY: *9 September*

In the late 16th century, the port of Cartagena in Colombia was the centre of a thriving slave trade. Thousands of captive Africans arrived at the port every month. Here, Peter Claver baptized about 300,000 enslaved people and ministered also to traders, sailors, prisoners and others in need.

Born in Catalonia in Spain and educated at the University of Barcelona, Peter Claver's spiritual journey began at the Jesuit college in Majorca. Here, he met Alphonsus Rodriguez, who foretold that they both had a future in South America.

Peter left for Cartagena in 1610, and was ordained there by the Jesuits five years later. Inspired by working alongside Father Alfonso de Sandoval, who had been ministering to the slaves for 40 years, Claver declared himself "the slave of Negroes forever".

Below Sts Peter Claver and Aloysius Gonzaga (St Xavier Church, Amsterdam, Holland).

Left A stained glass showing St Peter Claver (La Chapelle de La Colombière, Chalon sur Saône, France, 1930).

MISSIONARY TO THE SLAVES

Peter would meet the slave ships as they came into the harbour. Conscious of the need for immediate emotional and physical care, he comforted the slaves with his gentle manner and gave them gifts of medicines, food, brandy and lemons. He carried pictures to convey Christ's life and his promise of redemption explaining to his helpers, "we must speak to them with our hands before we try to speak to them with our lips". He later visited the plantations and mines where these slaves were put to work. Refusing the hospitality of the owners, who were not all happy to see him, he stayed in the slaves' quarters.

In 1650, Peter succumbed to a plague, which left him weak and incapacitated. He was confined to his cell. He was neglected by everyone until Dona Isabel de Urbina, who had funded his charities, came to his rescue, and with her sister nursed him. Four years later, Peter took mass before falling into a coma. The people of Cartagena, realizing they were losing an extraordinary priest, were anxious to kiss his hands. Even plantation owners sensed his greatness, and after his death his cell was stripped of relics. He was canonized, along with his friend Alphonsus Rodriguez, in 1888.

JOSEPH OF COPERTINO

CREDITED WITH POWERS OF LEVITATION, AS WELL AS WITH MANY
OTHER MIRACLES, THIS SIMPLE, THOUGH MISUNDERSTOOD, PRIEST
GAINED THE NICKNAME "THE FLYING FRIAR".

KEY FACTS
Mystic, miracle worker
DATES: *1603–63*
BIRTH PLACE: *Copertino, near
Brindisi, Italy*
PATRON OF: *Aviation,
astronauts, students and students'
examinations*
FEAST DAY: *18 September*
EMBLEM: *Flying in Franciscan habit*

The story of Joseph of Copertino is a sad one. His father's death left his mother penniless and she considered the slow-witted Joseph a tiresome burden. He was widely ridiculed and known for his violent temper. He seemed incapable of learning a trade and was rejected by local monasteries until Franciscans at Grottella accepted him as a servant. The young boy became serious in his devotions and performed menial tasks without complaint.

Despite his academic struggles, Joseph was ordained in 1628 and legends began to surround him. The mere sight of religious imagery or the mention of holy names sent Joseph into a state of ecstasy during which his body would rise in the air.

Above Pope Urban VIII *(Gianlorenzo Bernini, c.1625–30), before whom Joseph experienced a religious ecstasy.*

Below St Joseph of Copertino levitates in front of an image of the Virgin. The saint was known for such ecstasies.

INQUISITION AND EXILE

In Joseph's 17 years at Grottella, witnesses recorded 70 incidents of levitation. One extraordinary occurrence reportedly took place during the construction of a cross of Calvary. The centre strut was 11m/36ft high and very heavy. Ten men couldn't lift it, but during the night, Joseph flew through the air, raised the strut and fixed it to the earth.

This behaviour so worried his superiors that he was prohibited from celebrating mass, eating with his brethren or attending processions. As his trances continued, and the public interest in him increased, Joseph was taken for questioning by the Inquisitors in Naples. Finding no fault with him, they sent him to Rome, where, at an audience with Pope Urban VIII, Joseph fell into an ecstasy and the pope decided to send him to Assisi.

With crowds of people seeking out the "Flying Friar", Joseph was exiled to a monastery at Pietrarossa, and was forbidden to speak or write to anyone. When pilgrims continued to clamour for a glimpse of his miracles, he was sent to an even more remote monastery at Fossombrone, and then to Assisi, where he was kept in strict isolation. Although consoled by his visions, Joseph died in solitude. In 1767, he was canonized for his humility and patience.

VINCENT DE PAUL

A CLEVER AND DIPLOMATIC FRENCH PRIEST, ADEPT AT PERSUADING
THE WEALTHY TO BE GENEROUS TO THE POOR. TODAY, HIS SOCIETIES
CONTINUE HIS TRADITION OF CHARITY AND SOCIAL WELFARE.

KEY FACTS
*Founder of charitable orders,
hospitals and orphanages*
DATES: *1581–1660*
BIRTH PLACE: *Landes, France*
PATRON OF: *Charity workers,
hospitals, prisoners, Madagascar*
FEAST DAY: *27 September*
EMBLEM: *White cloak,
begging bowl*

Vincent de Paul was born in Gascony to a peasant family, but he escaped the harsh life of a farmer by studying under the Franciscans at Dax and later attending Toulouse University. He was ordained at 19 and undertook a journey to Rome, at which point he seemed to vanish for two years. Historians suspect that he obscured, or even invented, the truth about this time.

In fact, Vincent himself perpetuated the most famous account of these two years through letters he wrote to his patron, a Gascon judge called Monsieur de Comet. He claimed that, on his way from

Above St Vincent de Paul *(attributed to Daniel Dumonstier, 17th century).*

Below St Vincent de Paul and the Sisters of Charity *(Jean Andre, c.1729).*

Toulouse to Narbonne, his ship was overwhelmed by Barbary pirates. He was sold into slavery at Tunis and endured two years there before, appealing to the Christian faith of one of his captors, he managed to escape to Marseilles.

Following this uncertain period, Vincent appeared in Rome, where he was given instructions by Pope Paul V to travel to the French court of Henry IV. Vincent remained in Paris as chaplain to the queen, which gave him access to the rich and powerful members of court. He was charming and kind and able to persuade many wealthy patrons to devote funds to his worthy causes.

CHARITY WORKER

Vincent's sensitivities to the suffering of others came to dominate his thinking. He met, and was profoundly influenced by, Francis of Sales, and expanded his work to found hospitals and orphanages. He also worked to improve the lives of galley slaves and gave missions to prisoners in Bordeaux.

Then, in 1625, he founded an order of priests to preach in remote villages, where they cared for convicts and the poor. From 1633, the men lived in small communal groups and became known as the Vincentians, or Lazarists. The order was so successful in its mission that the Archbishop of Paris

Above An old people's home run by the Sisters of Charity at St Vincent de Paul's hospital in Peking (1900).

asked Vincent to train priests for parish work. For 27 years, Vincent gave weekly conferences, and his priests taught at seminaries around France. They also travelled as missionaries to Madagascar, Poland, Ireland, Scotland and countries in Africa.

Also in 1633, Vincent asked his friend, Louise de Marillac, to help him form an order of women to nurse the sick. At this time, nuns lived in enclosed houses, cut off from public lives. This new order, the Sisters of Charity, took a vow of obedience for one year only,

"IT IS OUR DUTY TO PREFER THE SERVICE OF THE POOR TO EVERY-THING ELSE, AND TO OFFER SUCH SERVICE AS QUICKLY AS POSSIBLE... OFFER THE DEED TO GOD AS YOUR PRAYER."

ST VINCENT DE PAUL

this being the time the Church allowed noviciates to enjoy social contact. They renewed their vows yearly, but Vincent's rule allowed them to take their good works into the wider world.

INFLUENCE

Vincent de Paul had a profound effect on Church reform and was extremely popular and influential in his lifetime. He inspired countless men and women to care for the dispossessed, and the rich to fund the work. His Sisters of Charity and Vincentians continue to work all around the world, helping the homeless, the debt-ridden, orphans and prisoners. In 1833, Frederick Ozanam, a Frenchman, instituted a lay brotherhood in the name of Saint Vincent de Paul. The modern worldwide membership of SVP, as this charity is called, includes men and women, Catholics and

LOUISE DE MARILLAC

When Louise de Marillac was widowed in 1625, she devoted herself to the charity work of Vincent de Paul. He depended on her good sense, and she helped found the Sisters of Charity, "whose convent is the sickroom; their chapel their parish church; their cloister, the city streets". She was an inspiring teacher and, under her guidance, women were committed to 40 houses of the Charity, working with the sick and giving shelter to distressed women. She was canonized in 1934. Her feast day is 15 March.

Above Louise de Marillac distributing alms to the poor (Diogène Maillart, 1920).

Protestants. Vincent always insisted that Protestants be treated with courtesy and understanding.

Vincent's teaching of care and service, his gentle faith, and resolute belief in the sustaining love of God brought him many friends and admirers. He died peacefully and was buried at the church of Saint-Lazare. He was beatified in 1729 and Pope Clement XII canonized him in 1737.

Above The Church of St Vincent de Paul in Paris (*Rouargue Frères, 19th century*).

MARGUERITE BOURGEOYS

THIS PIONEERING EDUCATOR, WHO ESTABLISHED THE FIRST RELIGIOUS ORDER IN CANADA AND THE FIRST SCHOOL IN MONTREAL, BECAME KNOWN AS THE "MOTHER OF THE COLONY".

KEY FACTS

Educator, founder of a religious order
DATES: *1620–1700*
BIRTH PLACE: *Troyes, France*
PATRON OF: *Poverty*
FEAST DAY: *12 January*

Born into the large family of a rich merchant, Marguerite Bourgeoys enjoyed a privileged upbringing. After her mother's death in 1639, she cared for her younger siblings but soon felt the calling of a religious vocation.

She joined a lay order of women called the Congregation of Troyes, an organization devoted to teaching the poor children of the area.

CALLED TO CANADA

In 1652, Marguerite's future took a dramatic turn when she met Monsieur de Maisonneuve, a governor in New France (now Canada). He was recruiting teachers for an outpost called Ville-Marie, and because she was not a cloistered nun, Marguerite was able to accept the challenge.

She arrived at the fort in 1653, finding herself both teacher and nurse for the tiny community. As there was no permanent place of

Above An engraving of a tattooed Iroquois Indian holding a snake and smoking a peace pipe (c.1701).

Below Marguerite Bourgeoys with Canadian Indian converts (artist and date unknown).

worship, she organized the building of the stone chapel of Notre-Dame-de-Bon-Secour in 1655. A year later, seeing an urgent need for education in this new land, she established the first Montreal school, teaching domestic, spiritual and academic subjects. The school thrived and she travelled back to France three times in the following years to enlist teachers.

FOUNDING EDUCATOR

Marguerite and her fellow teachers were very courageous women, spreading their schools across the wilderness of Quebec. They were resolved to educate the children of the Iroquois tribes as well as those of the French colonists, but they faced hardships of illness, hunger, fires, and violent attacks from the very people they hoped to help. In 1676, determined to persevere with her cause, Marguerite founded the Sisters of Notre Dame.

Sadly, by 1698, she had become exhausted by hardship, and chose to resign as the superior. In keeping with the selflessness of her life, she nursed a young nun who was dying. She prayed, "God, why do you not take me instead, I who am useless and good for nought!" The young nun lived and, a few days later, Marguerite died. Thousands mourned the loss of her wise, steady guidance.

Today, giving testimony to her faith and ambition, there are 200 convents and missions around the world following Marguerite's ideals of Christian education.

LOUIS GRIGNION DE MONTFORT

THIS UNCONVENTIONAL PRIEST ENRAGED CHURCH AUTHORITIES BUT HIS MISSIONS TO THE POOR AND INSPIRATIONAL SERMONS ENSURED HIM RECOGNITION AS A FAITHFUL APOSTLE.

KEY FACTS
Missionary apostolic and founder
DATES: *1673–1716*
BIRTH PLACE: *Montfort, Brittany*
FEAST DAY: *28 April*

As a student in Paris, Louis de Montfort experienced such squalid poverty that his future course as a missionary to the poor was decided. After his ordination in Paris in 1700, he was sent to work in Poitiers. There he founded the Daughters of Wisdom, an order of nuns that nursed in hospitals, and took his own mission to the poorest quarters.

EVANGELIST TO THE POOR
He was very popular with the public, but his flamboyant speeches caused concern among his superiors. To enhance his lessons, Louis would make an effigy of the devil dressed as a rich woman, then burn irreligious books before it. Or he would act out the role of a dying sinner caught between the angels and the devil. His writing, too, was dramatic. The *True Devotion to the Blessed Virgin* gained a wide readership, except among theologians.

Banned from Poitiers for his evangelistic style, Louis was given the office of "missionary apostolic" by the pope. This allowed him to roam Brittany and Poitiers, which well suited his personality. The singing of the hymns that he wrote reinforced his intense and emotional preaching, and he encouraged the use of the rosary in prayer.

Right Pope Pius XII canonized Louis Grignion de Montfort in 1947.

Wherever he went, churches were restored and charity to the poor was revived. Lapsed believers returned to faith after attending his sermons, while in La Rochelle, a number of Calvinists returned to the Roman Catholic Church.

In 1712, Louis founded an association of missionary priests called the Company of

Above Louis Grignion de Montfort in a church dedicated to him in Saint-Laurent-sur-Sèvres.

Mary. These men, and the women of his Daughters of Wisdom, were trained to follow his emotional approach to faith. The orders have since become highly successful international apostolic and educational missions.

Louis Grignion de Montfort died in Saint-Laurent-sur-Sèvres and was canonized in 1947.

JEANNE DELANOUE

JEANNE DELANOUE GAVE UP A BUSY COMMERCIAL LIFE FOR ONE OF PERSONAL SQUALOR, DEVOTING HER LIFE INSTEAD TO CARING FOR THE POOR, PARTICULARLY OUTCAST WOMEN AND REFUGEES.

KEY FACTS
Founder
DATES: *1666–1736*
BIRTH PLACE: *Saumur, France*
FEAST DAY: *17 August*

In her earlier life, Jeanne Delanoue ran the family business, selling drapery and religious items. At the age of 26, she encountered Françoise Suchet, a religious enthusiast who claimed to have experienced visions. Inspired by this eccentric woman, Jeanne turned her home and shop into a guesthouse, transforming the cellars and caves below it into shelters for the homeless.

By 1704, Jeanne had founded an order that came to be called the Sisters of Providence. The order brought solace to homeless women, unmarried mothers, and prostitutes, and during the famine

Right The Castle in Saumur, the city where Jeanne Delanoue was born and founded her religious order.

of 1709 they housed 100 starving people. Each day, having slept in a filthy old shroud, Jeanne would rise at 3 a.m., pray, then tend to the needy women.

Her nickname, "the pig of Jesus", suggests a lack of care for her appearance, but Jeanne was greatly respected for her protection of outcasts, and for her care of refugees during the frequent periods of war and famine. She founded 12 communities before her death in Saumur.

FRANCIS SERRANO

A COURAGEOUS AND FAITHFUL MISSIONARY, FRANCIS SERRANO WAS COMPLIMENTED BY A FELLOW PRIEST FOR WORKING "AS ENERGETICALLY AS A LION FOR THE BENEFIT OF SOULS".

KEY FACTS
Martyr
DATES: *1691–1748*
BIRTH PLACE: *Granada, Spain*
FEAST DAY: *17 February*

Francis Serrano was a Dominican priest who left Spain for the Philippines in 1725. Assigned to the post of Fujian, he showed great virtue as a missionary in a treacherous land.

Serrano was a hardy man, who had an abundance of energy, and was adventurous in spirit. His writings reveal him as a humorous, high-spirited character. He would journey unafraid through the night, crossing rivers and forests, determined to tend to his persecuted flock. He even disguised himself as a local peasant

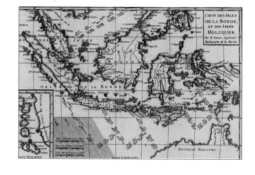

so that he could pass unnoticed into villages to administer the Sacraments in secret.

In 1746, he was imprisoned in Fuzhou and, during 19 months of incarceration, endured violent

Left A map of Indonesia and the Philippines (Charles Marie Rigobert Bonne, 18th century).

beatings that badly damaged his hearing. He and other missionaries were branded on their faces, and Francis wrote, "Our hearts exulted. We were branded as slaves of Jesus Christ...these heads are no longer ours, but the Lord's. He can take them whenever He wishes." Francis, who was finally suffocated to death in his prison cell, is included among the Martyrs of China canonized in 2000.

LEONARD OF PORT MAURICE

LEONARD WISHED FIRST, THAT HE "MIGHT LIVE FOR GOD AND LAST, THAT HE MIGHT LIVE IN GOD". TRAVELLING AROUND ITALY, HE USED THE STATIONS OF THE CROSS TO PREACH THE CHRISTIAN MESSAGE.

KEY FACTS
Franciscan missionary
DATES: *1676–1751*
BIRTH PLACE: *Port Maurice, Italy*
PATRON OF: *Missions in
Catholic lands*
FEAST DAY: *26 November*
EMBLEM: *Franciscan habit*

Baptized as Paul Jerome Casanova in Port Maurice, Leonard joined the Franciscan Order, basing his life on the teachings of Christ as he understood them from a close reading of the New Testament, and on the Rules of St Francis of Assisi.

In 1709, Leonard instituted reforms at the friary of San Francesco del Monte in Florence, bringing its practices back into line with the strict austerity demanded by St Francis. He attracted many followers, whom he trained and sent out to preach across Tuscany. He also established a hermitage nearby, with the purpose of enabling the friars to make biannual retreats of silence and fasting. In 1730, he was sent to Rome, where he was appointed Guardian of St Bonaventura. During his time here, he made a point of ministering to soldiers, sailors, convicts and galley slaves.

STATIONS OF THE CROSS
In 1736, Leonard asked to be released from office, and travelled around Italy, often preaching outdoors. As a tool to spread his message, and as a symbol of his devotion, he used the Stations of the Cross, teaching his listeners how to pray before each of the

Left Leonard of Port Maurice used the Stations of the Cross to teach his listeners about the Christian faith. The Fifth Station recounts how Simon of Cyrene helped Christ carry the cross (Giovanni Domenico Tiepolo, 1749).

14 incidents that marked Christ's journey to the cross. It is said that he installed about 500 Stations of the Cross throughout Italy.

In 1744, Pope Benedict XIV sent Leonard to Corsica, where he encountered a hostile political atmosphere, and turbulent congregations who brought weapons to church services. The mountainous land was hard for a priest, who had to walk everywhere. Leonard's health suffered, and eventually, a ship had to be sent to bring him home.

Leonard returned to his Italian flock with renewed vigour and, in 1750, set up the Stations of the Cross in the Roman Coliseum, where he preached to a huge, excited crowd.

Soon afterward, he took a mission to the south, but the weather turned against him. Refusing an offer of shelter from some friars at Spoleto, Leonard insisted on continuing to Rome. Here he took to his bed and, exhausted by the journey, he received the last rites and a message from the pope before he died.

Left The Gulf of Porto in Corsica. Leonard was sent to the island by Pope Benedict XIV in 1744.

GERARD MAJELLA

GERARD MAJELLA, A HUMBLE, SIMPLE LAY BROTHER FROM A MODEST BACKGROUND, HAS BEEN DESCRIBED AS THE "MOST FAMOUS WONDER-WORKER OF THE 18TH CENTURY".

KEY FACTS
Miracle worker
DATES: *1725–55*
BIRTH PLACE: *Muro Lucano, near Naples*
PATRON OF: *Mothers*
FEAST DAY: *16 October*

Gerard Majella's widowed mother said of him that "he was born for heaven", and he demonstrated his religious calling from an early age, spending much of his childhood in prayer.

He initially turned down an apprenticeship as a tailor – his father's profession – to work as a servant in the house of the Bishop of Lacedogna. But the bishop was bad-tempered and unpredictable, and Gerard was neither sly nor subtle enough to withstand such a regime. So he returned home to take up his apprenticeship and worked to support his mother and three sisters.

A SIMPLE LAY BROTHER

In 1752, Gerard fulfilled his long-held dream to join a religious order when he was accepted as a lay brother into the Congregation of the Most Holy Redeemer, or the Redemptorists. St Alphonsus

Above Gerard Majella saving fishermen near Naples (M. Barberis, 19th century).

Below The Market at Naples (Domenico Gargiulo, 17th century). Gerard Majella never travelled beyond the boundaries of the city.

Liguori, the founder of this community, had a particular empathy with peasant and illiterate congregations and Gerard found a role as a gardener, tailor and porter. His fellow priests were puzzled by his frail appearance and shy manners, and decided that he must be "either a fool or a great saint".

MIRACLES AND CHARITY

Claims were soon circulating that Gerard could heal the sick, appear in two places at one time, read minds and tell the future. Perhaps most extraordinary of all, one story tells of his ability to levitate and fly half a mile through the air.

Despite Gerard's lowly position in the Redemptorists, he always found alms and food for the poor, and time and patience for the sick. Because of his purity and sensitivity, he was appointed as the spiritual director of numerous communities of nuns.

He remained unworldly and, when accused of lewd behaviour by a young woman, refused to defend or incriminate himself, believing silence to be the righteous response to dishonesty and injustice. The girl later admitted that the charges were false.

Gerard was only 29 years old when he died of tuberculosis. Although he had never travelled outside the kingdom of Naples, a cultus grew after his death. He is patron saint of unborn children and expectant mothers in particular, and was canonized by Pope Pius X in 1904.

MARGARET D'YOUVILLE

MARGARET D'YOUVILLE IS KNOWN AS THE MOTHER OF UNIVERSAL CHARITY. THE FOUNDER OF THE SISTERS OF CHARITY OF MONTREAL, SHE "LOVED GREATLY JESUS CHRIST AND THE POOR".

KEY FACTS
Founder
DATES: *1701–71*
BIRTH PLACE: *Varennes, Canada*
FEAST DAY: *23 December*

From a very early age, Margaret was faced with responsibility and the rigours of poverty. Born in Varennes, Canada, she was the eldest of six children. Her father died when she was seven years old and, after a brief education from the Ursuline nuns, she helped her mother to bring up her siblings.

From this difficult start in life, she made what appeared to be a good marriage to a fur trader, François Youville. The Governor-General and other grand officials attended the wedding.

Margaret's marriage brought her great unhappiness, during which her faith sustained her. Youville was not only a drunkard and a gambler, but also illicitly traded alcohol with local Indians. The effect of this was so devastating on their community that they begged the governor for protection. Margaret bore four children, of whom only two survived. When her husband died in 1730, she found he had spent her mother's legacy and left her in debt.

DEVOTION TO THE POOR
Margaret opened a shop to support her children and, despite her own hardships, found time to visit others in unfortunate circumstances. She tended to the sick and to criminals and, when her eldest son left home to enter the seminary (both sons became priests), she moved a destitute blind woman into his room. Her female

Right Montreal on the St Lawrence River in 1760. *Margaret founded her order in the city in 1737.*

friends shared her sense of duty and faith and worked as seamstresses to raise money for the poor. But Margaret still struggled to find resources to pay for her good works. She was once forced to beg for funds to pay for the funeral of an executed criminal.

Left The Storming of Quebec *(English School, 18th century). The "Grey Nuns" tended the wounded on both sides of the fighting.*

THE GREY NUNS
In 1737, along with three young companions, Margaret formed a lay order for the service of the poor – the Sisters of Charity of Montreal, known as the "Grey Nuns". They cared for women and prisoners, nursed the sick during a smallpox epidemic, and with an all-embracing policy that made no distinction of race or status, they tended to the wounded of both sides during the war between Quebec and England that ended in 1759. The Grey Nuns' convent was burnt down twice, but the entire community funded the rebuilding.

Margaret died in Montreal, and was canonized in 1990, the first native-born Canadian saint.

ANTÔNIO DE SANT'ANNA GALVÃO

MORE THAN A MILLION PEOPLE ATTENDED THE CANONIZATION OF ST ANTÔNIO, A MAN OF PEACE AND CHARITY, AND THE FIRST BRAZILIAN TO BE MADE A SAINT.

KEY FACTS
Founder, miracle worker
DATES: *1739–1822*
BIRTH PLACE: *Guaratingueto, near São Paulo, Brazil*
FEAST DAY: *11 May*

Antônio de Sant'Anna Galvão was born into a wealthy and deeply religious family, who sent him to a Jesuit seminary at the age of 13. However, because of a strong anti-Jesuit movement in Brazil at the time, his father advised him to join the Alcantrine Franciscans.

Antônio enrolled as a noviciate at St Bonaventure near Rio de Janeiro and was ordained in 1762. In 1768, he became preacher and confessor to the laity at the St Francis Friary in São Paulo. He was also confessor to the women of the Recollects of St Teresa, where he met Sister Helena Maria of the Holy Spirit.

In 1774, inspired by this nun and her religious visions, he founded Our Lady of the Conception of Divine Providence. At this home for girls, young women could receive instruction without being required to take vows. When Sister Helena died, Antônio took sole responsibility for the

***Above** An altar painting of Antônio de Sant'Anna Galvão in Brazil.*

***Below** Pope Benedict XVI canonized Antônio de Sant'Anna Galvão in front of nearly a million people in São Paulo in May 2007.*

Recollects, who were subsequently incorporated into the Order of Immaculate Conception.

Over the following years, Antônio achieved high office. In 1808, he became visitator in general and president of the Franciscan Chapter of São Paulo. When, at one stage, the Church posted him outside the city, the bishop and churchgoers begged for his return.

In his old age, he returned to the St Francis Friary, but it was the sisters from the Recollects da Luz who attended him at his death.

MIRACLE PILLS

Antônio is most famous for his "pills" – scraps of paper inscribed with prayers to Mary, the Blessed Virgin, that the faithful would swallow in hope of a miraculous cure. To this day, the pills are manufactured by the nuns of St Clare, a convent founded by Antônio in Sorocaba near São Paulo.

In 1998, the Archbishop of São Paulo tried to bring an end to what he regarded as a superstition, and ordered the nuns to stop their work. However, at the canonization of St Antônio, Pope Benedict XVI recognized the miraculous power of the saint, acknowledging two healing miracles ascribed to the pills, including a recent case of a four-year-old girl whose hepatitis had been declared incurable by the medical profession. Since the saint's canonization in 2007, the nuns have distributed as many as 10,000 pills in one day.

MAGDALENA OF CANOSSA

MAGDALENA OF CANOSSA HAD "A MOTHER'S HEART AND AN APOSTLE'S ZEAL". HER LIFE WAS DEDICATED TO TEACHING AND EXTENDING SPIRITUAL AWARENESS.

KEY FACTS
*Virgin, founder of the
Daughters of Charity*
DATES: *1774–1835*
BIRTH PLACE: *Verona, Italy*
FEAST DAY: *8 May*

Although Magdalena made a vow to dedicate her life to God at the age of 17, she was compelled to take up a secular life. The third of six siblings left fatherless as children, she found herself in charge of running the family's large estate.

Despite her worldly worries, however, she could not forget her calling, and sought out friends to join her in following Christ with chastity and obedience. In 1808, in spite of family opposition, she moved to the poorest part of town to start her religious life, and built up such a following that, in 1819, she founded the Daughters of Charity. The order was dedicated to establishing charity schools, training teachers for rural areas and supporting women patients in hospital. Later, she founded the Sons of Charity for male followers.

Magdalena died in Verona surrounded by her followers. There are now 4,000 Daughters of Charity all over the world, and the Sons are active in Italy, the Philippines and Latin America.

Above St Mary's College in Hong Kong, founded by the Canossian Daughters of Charity in 1900.

JOSEPH COTTOLENGO

JOSEPH COTTOLENGO WILL ALWAYS BE REMEMBERED AND LOVED AS AN UNSTINTING CHAMPION OF THOSE IN NEED, WHETHER THEY BE ORPHANS, DISABLED, MENTALLY ILL OR FRAIL.

KEY FACTS
Founder
DATES: *1786–1842*
BIRTH PLACE: *Piedmont*
FEAST DAY: *30 April*

Joseph Cottolengo was ordained in 1811 and quickly demonstrated his empathy for the unfortunate. His good works began modestly, with the founding of a hospital of five beds, the "Little House", in a Turin slum.

The hospital expanded quickly, and Joseph and his followers formed the Societies of the Little House of Divine Providence. When the authorities closed the Little House during a cholera epidemic, the brothers nursed the sick in their homes. The Little House then moved to Valdocco, a suburb of Turin, where it was soon

Above The city of Turin, where Joseph Cottolengo did many great works.

surrounded by an assortment of care homes for the deaf and dumb, orphans, elderly people, epileptics and the mentally handicapped.

Joseph also started communities of prayer to bring solace to those in mortal and moral danger. Joseph seemed carefree about finances, believing that the Lord would provide, and so it was with surprise that his successor accepted his perfectly kept account books when he retired.

Although he was only 56 years old, Joseph died of typhoid in his brother's home at Chieri only a week after his retirement.

CHARLES LWANGA

CHARLES LWANGA, ONE OF THE NAMED MARTYRS OF UGANDA, WAS MURDERED BECAUSE HE PROTECTED THE CHILDREN IN HIS CARE AND REFUSED TO DENY HIS FAITH.

KEY FACTS
Martyr of Uganda
DATES: *1865–86*
BIRTH PLACE: *Uganda*
FEAST DAY: *3 June*

The tyrant of Uganda, King Mwanga, beheaded the bishop missionary James Hannington and the Ugandan convert Joseph Mkasa, but he did not stop there.

When Mwanga killed a page, Denis Sebuggwawo, for teaching the catechism, Charles Lwanga, who supervised the court pages, voiced his rage. That night, fearing the worst, Lwanga baptized four of the boys in his charge.

In the morning, the King called up Charles Lwanga, 15 pages and numerous other Christians captured by his warriors. He told

Above The Martyrs Monument at Namugongo in Uganda, which commemorates the martyrdom of Christians on 3 June 1886.

them to deny their faith but they said they would remain Christians "until death". They were marched to Namugongo, where they were beaten, wrapped in reed mats and burnt alive. Their joyful courage has been likened to that of the early Christians.

Mwanga murdered many more Christians, including Matthias Murumba and Andrew Kagwa. In 1964, 22 of the young men, including Charles Lwanga, were canonized as the Martyrs of Uganda. Their feast day is a public holiday in Uganda.

MARIE ADOLPHINE DIERKS

MARIE ADOLPHINE DIERKS WAS A HUMBLE DUTCH WOMAN WHO FELT CALLED UPON AND COMPELLED BY GOD TO BECOME A NUN. SHE SAID, "I WANT TO SUFFER FOR THE LORD".

KEY FACTS
Martyr of China
DATES: *1866–1900*
BIRTH PLACE: *Ossendrecht, Holland*
FEAST DAY: *17 February*

Marie was born in Holland, one of six siblings who lost their mother at an early age and were taken in by poor but kindly neighbours. Marie was dedicated to her studies and her prayers, but soon realized that her adoptive family needed financial help. She worked as a factory hand and as a domestic servant, giving part of her earnings to her family.

However, she felt a strong call to serve God, and in 1893 she joined the Franciscan Missionaries of Mary in Antwerp. With six other nuns, she was sent to the

Left A colour lithograph depicting the murder of a nun during the Boxer Rebellion in China.

Shanxi diocese in China. Work at the hospital and orphanage in Shanxi was hard, but Marie served with patience.

She was beheaded, along with her six Christian colleagues, in a crackdown on foreign missionaries during the Boxer Rebellion of 1900. Her name is included in the list of the 120 Blessed Martyrs of China, canonized by Pope John Paul II in 2000.

JOHN BOSCO

JOHN BOSCO WAS A GREAT TEACHER WHO NEVER PUNISHED HIS PUPILS BUT, INSTEAD, GUIDED BY A CHILDHOOD VISION, USED THE "PREVENTIVE" MEASURES OF LOVE, PATIENCE AND FIRMNESS.

KEY FACTS
Founder
DATES: *1815–88*
BIRTH PLACE: *Piedmont, Italy*
PATRON OF: *Editors, young people, young workers, apprentices and youth of Mexico*
FEAST DAY: *31 January*

John Bosco's life was given direction by a dream he had when he was very young. In this dream, he saw a group of young boys who were playing and swearing. To stop their blaspheming he punched them with his fists, but a man intervened, saying "You will have to win these friends of yours not by blows, but by gentleness and love."

A LIFE OF POVERTY

John was born into a peasant family from Piedmont, Italy, but lost his father when he was only two years old. He was brought up by his mother, and such was their poverty that, when he decided to enter a seminary in 1831, his clothes and shoes were donated by neighbours.

After he was ordained priest in 1841, John became chaplain of a girl's school in Turin. On Sundays, a group of boys who lived on the city streets would come to the school to play and learn their catechism. John quickly realized, with the help of his guide and teacher, Joseph Cafasso, that his life's work lay with these boys.

LED BY HIS DREAM

Bosco left the school and went to live in shabby rooms in the Valdocco area of Turin, where, with his mother as housekeeper, he housed and educated the abandoned boys of the city. He set up shoemaking, tailoring and printing workshops, where the boys could learn a trade, and gave them lessons in Latin and grammar. Never forgetting his dream, Bosco

Above A mosaic tile depiction of St John Bosco in Seville, Spain.

fostered a good relationship with his pupils through recreation, and encouraged picnics, outdoor play and a love of nature and music.

By 1856, he was housing 150 boys and he began to train likeminded people to help him in his work. He called these teachers

"Salesians", after St Francis of Sales. They were approved as a religious order in 1874.

Bosco founded a similar order for women – the Daughters of Our Lady, Help of Christians – in 1872. These orders are now established across the globe, and run seminaries and technical and agricultural colleges.

John Bosco died in 1888, shortly after the completion of his church dedicated to the Sacred Heart in Rome, where he had been able to offer only one mass. About 40,000 mourners visited his body and the people of Turin lined the streets to watch the cortège. He was canonized by Pope Pius XI in 1934.

Below Part of an engraving from an Italian newspaper showing the canonization of John Bosco in St Peter's in 1934.

THERESA OF LISIEUX

THERESA, THE "LITTLE FLOWER", WROTE OF HER RELATIONSHIP WITH GOD WITH AN ARTLESS SIMPLICITY THAT CONVEYED A DEEP SPIRITUALITY, QUALIFYING HER AS A DOCTOR OF THE CHURCH.

KEY FACTS
Virgin, mystic, Doctor of the Church
DATES: *1873–1897*
BIRTH PLACE: *Alençon, France*
PATRON OF: *France, missions, florists and flower growers*
FEAST DAY: *1 October*
EMBLEM: *Flowers*

Theresa of Lisieux lived a very ordinary life. She did not perform great works, found a religious order or convert thousands to Christianity. And yet this young girl, who lived for such a brief time, left a rich spiritual legacy.

AN EARLY VOCATION

Although she was only four years old when her mother died, Theresa had four older sisters to look after her. The eldest, Pauline, became her surrogate mother, but by the time Theresa was ten, her two eldest sisters had left home to enter the local Carmelite convent in Lisieux.

Theresa begged constantly to join the convent, but she was too young to take such vows. On a pilgrimage to Rome with her father, she knelt for a blessing

Above Theresa of Lisieux (artist and date unknown). Aware she was dying, Theresa wrote that, after her death, she would "let fall a shower of roses", meaning that in heaven she would intercede for her friends.

from Pope Leo XIII. Knowing that she was forbidden to speak to him, she broke all protocol and begged him to let her be a nun. He supported the decision of the Carmelites, but when Theresa reached the age of 15, the Bishop of Bayeux, impressed by her piety and determination, allowed the prioress to admit her.

In April 1888, the young girl began her life in the enclosed Carmelite convent, where she began to develop her spirituality by reading the Carmelite mystics and following the austere rules of the order. The abbess forbade

Left A photograph of Theresa of Lisieux in the garden of the Carmelite convent in Lisieux in France (c.1890).

Theresa to fast because she was not physically robust, but she sensed that the young girl was an intuitive thinker, and encouraged her to write. This wise advice allowed Theresa the time and space to produce *The Story of a Soul*, and her many other texts, which include 54 poems, 20 prayers, eight plays and more than 200 letters. In a simple poetic style, these writings describe how every "little life" can be enhanced by faith and reveal her extraordinary relationship with God.

THE "LITTLE WAY"

The young nun longed to be a saint, but aware that, as a Carmelite, she would not be able to achieve great works, she looked for a new path that would lead her to sanctity. "I knew I was a very little soul who could offer only little things to the good God", she wrote. From this thought grew her "little way" of "the doing of the least actions for love".

A year after she had joined the Carmelites, Theresa's father suffered two strokes that left him weak and dependent. Emotionally disturbed and unhappy, he had a nervous breakdown, and in 1894, died in a lunatic asylum. Her fourth sister, Celine, who had spent her life caring for their father, joined Theresa at the Carmelite convent.

Theresa wanted to follow the example of the apostles and

Above The Basilica of St Theresa in Lisieux, France, is the saint's major shrine.

longed for the opportunity to spread the love of Christ in foreign lands. She had always prayed for missionaries – it was a Carmelite discipline to pray for Christian missions abroad – but she also corresponded with the Carmelite nuns in Hanoi, Indo-China (now Vietnam), and they wanted her to join them.

QUIET SUFFERING

Then, in 1895, Theresa had a curious experience. During the night between Maundy Thursday and Good Friday, she heard "as it were, a far-off murmur announcing the coming of the Bridegroom". She seemed unaware that she was bleeding from her mouth – a symptom of tuberculosis. With her health broken, her dream of becoming a missionary would never be realized.

For 18 months, Theresa suffered pain and difficulty in breathing. She was eventually confined to the convent infirmary, where she was so ill that she was unable to receive Holy Communion. She died at the age of 24.

Pilgrims still flock to Lisieux to venerate St Theresa, who is known as the "little flower of Jesus" and Theresa-of-the-Child-Jesus, names that reflect her simple, childlike faith. Her book has been translated into 50 languages and has brought inspiration to millions of people. Theresa of Lisieux was canonized in 1925.

Below St Theresa, from a cycle of Carmelite Life made from mosaic in the Basilica of St Theresa in Lisieux, France (Pierre Gaudin, 1958).

"I desire to be a saint, but I know my weakness and so I ask you, my God, that you yourself will be my holiness."

THERESA OF LISIEUX

GEMMA GALGANI

Born in 1878, Gemma was an orphan, terribly afflicted by tuberculosis of the spine. She resembled Theresa of Lisieux in other ways, too. Hers was a "little life" without office, wealth or public recognition. Faith guided all her actions, only ill health preventing her from entering a convent. Her mysticism was expressed in ecstasies, during which she gave spiritual messages. She had visions of Jesus and stigmata appeared on her body. Heroic in enduring illness and poverty, Gemma died in 1903 and was canonized in 1941.

Above Lucca in Tuscany, Italy. St Gemma Galgani's relics are housed at the Passionist monastery in the city.

RAPHAEL KALINOWSKI

IN HIS ROLE AS A PRIEST, RAPHAEL KALINOWSKI FOSTERED HOPES OF UNITING CHRISTIANS, THROUGH SPIRITUAL GUIDANCE, TO COMBAT THE GROWING POWER OF THE SECULAR STATE.

KEY FACTS
Carmelite
DATES: *1835–1907*
BIRTH PLACE: *Vilnius, Poland (now Lithuania)*
FEAST DAY: *15 November*

The 19th century in Europe is a story of industrialization, nationalism and secular politics. The life of Raphael Kalinowski reflects the period. Raised a devout Catholic, he became an engineer, working on the new Russian railways. While running a Sunday school at the fortress in Brest-Litovsk where he was a captain, he became increasingly aware of the state persecution of the Church, and of his native Poles.

When the Poles rose against the Russians in 1863, Raphael joined them and was soon taken prisoner. Few survived the forced

march to slave labour in Siberia, but Raphael was sustained by his faith and became spiritual leader to the prisoners. He was released ten years later.

Left Polish Insurrectionists of the 1863 Rebellion (*Stanislaus von Chlebowski, 19th century*).

Profoundly changed by his experiences in Siberia, Kalinowski joined the Carmelites, and in 1882, he was ordained priest at the monastery at Czerna, near Cracow, the last Carmelite brotherhood allowed in Poland.

Raphael strove to revive the Carmelites in Poland and to bring religious freedom to his oppressed countrymen. He died in Wadowice and was canonized in 1991.

MIGUEL CORDERO

MIGUEL CORDERO OF ECUADOR WAS A GIFTED TEACHER, WHO, THROUGH HIS TEACHING AND WRITINGS, SPREAD THE WORD OF JESUS ACROSS HIS COUNTRY.

KEY FACTS
de la Sallist
DATES: *1854–1910*
BIRTH PLACE: *Cuenca, Ecuador*
FEAST DAY: *9 February*

Miguel Cordero was physically disabled but intellectually precocious. In his thinking, he was a precise theologian, but his actions showed a man concerned with the welfare of his students and fellow priests.

The de la Salle Brothers (the international teaching order founded by St John-Baptist de la Salle) accepted Cordero when he was only 14, and a year later, sent him to Quito in Ecuador. He proved to be an outstanding teacher. At the age of 20, he published a Spanish grammar that became adopted nationwide, and later

Above Cuenca in Ecuador, birth place of Miguel Cordero. Cordero was the first Ecuadorian to be accepted into the de la Salle teaching order.

wrote other acclaimed textbooks, and translated a life of John-Baptist de La Salle.

The Ecuadorian government despised the Church, but in spite of the state's efforts to suppress religion, Cordero's fame as a holy teacher and writer spread.

In 1907, he was called to work in Belgium. However, the Belgian climate did not suit him and he was moved to Barcelona. When an anti-clerical revolution erupted in the city, Cordero had to be rescued by gunboat. He died in Premia del Mar, Spain, in 1910, and was canonized in 1984.

FRANCES CABRINI

A MISSIONARY AMONG ITALIAN IMMIGRANTS IN AMERICA, FRANCES IS KNOWN AS THE "MOTHER OF EMIGRANTS" FOR HER WORK TO KEEP THE FAITH ALIVE AMONG CHRISTIANS FAR FROM HOME.

KEY FACTS
Founder
DATES: *1850–1917*
BIRTH PLACE: *Sant' Angelo Lodigiano, near Pavia, Italy*
PATRON OF: *Migrants and emigrants*
FEAST DAY: *22 December*

Frances Cabrini was a missionary in the New World, but she did not work among the indigenous people. Instead, she was sent to revive the faith of Italian immigrants in America. Initially, she thought the mission unnecessary, believing all Italians to be as devout as her relatives.

Frances was the youngest of 13 children of northern Italian parents. After qualifying as a teacher, she tried to become a nun but was refused by two orders for health reasons. She was a tiny woman, barely 164cm/5ft tall, but a friendly priest, guessing at her

Above The body of Frances Cabrini lies in state in the chapel at the Mother Cabrini High School in New York City.

Left A statue of St Frances Cabrini in the National Shrine of the Immaculate Conception in Washington, DC.

inner strength, appealed to his bishop, who invited her to manage a small orphanage in Codogno, Lombardy. She remained there until the house closed.

THE MISSIONARY SISTERS

The bishop encouraged Frances to start her own missionary congregation. She gathered seven women who had worked with her at Codogno and founded the Missionary Sisters of the Sacred Heart, dedicated to the education of Christian girls.

Frances had always wanted to work in China, but the Archbishop of New York had invited her to set up schools and orphanages for Italian immigrants. When, in 1889, she and six sisters crossed the Atlantic, they found no one had prepared for their arrival, and they had to live in poverty with the immigrants until Frances was able to find a building and open the orphanage.

SPREAD OF THE MISSION

Success followed, and Frances opened more orphanages and schools in New York. She also founded schools in Managua, the capital of Nicaragua, and in New Orleans. Over the following years, her mission spread to Italy, Costa Rica, Panama, Chile, Brazil, France and England. Her profound faith drove her, and her proudest achievement was in opening the Columbus Hospital in New York.

Before moving to the United States, Frances had never met a Protestant and had difficulty in accepting that they, too, could be Christian. Her views were stern on subjects such as illegitimacy, but her deep love of God and a sense of justice tempered her thinking and ideas.

When her Missionary Sisters of the Sacred Heart were approved in 1907, there were 1,000 members in eight countries, and they served orphans, schools, prisons and hospitals.

Frances died in Chicago in 1917 and, in 1946, was the first American to be canonized.

TERESA OF LOS ANDES

TERESA WANTED TO DEVOTE HER LIFE COMPLETELY TO JESUS AND "TO LOVE AND SUFFER FOR THE SALVATION OF SOULS". THE SIMPLE FAITH OF THIS YOUNG WOMAN HAS BECOME AN EXAMPLE TO MANY.

KEY FACTS
Virgin, Carmelite
DATES: *1900–20*
BIRTH PLACE: *Santiago, Chile*
FEAST DAY: *12 April*

The shrine of St Teresa of Los Andes at La Riconda attracts 100,000 pilgrims every year. She is among those pious young women, such as Theresa of Lisieux, whose every thought and action was directed toward God.

CALLED TO SUFFER

One of six children born in Santiago, Chile, to wealthy, unassuming Christian parents, Teresa was well educated in the sciences, music and the arts. Her parents, who named her Juanita, were pleased by the religious faith of their daughter and the happiness it seemed to bring her.

When she was 14 years old, and suffering a painful bout of appendicitis, Teresa heard the voice of Jesus telling her that her pain was in imitation of his suffering. She had been lively and athletic until then, nicknamed "the Amazon" by her brothers, but after hearing

Above A statue of St Teresa of Los Andes in Chile. A cultus developed after her death and she remains popular, especially with young women.

Jesus speak, she made an inner vow of chastity, took to teaching the catechism to deprived children, and read the biographies of Theresa of Avila and of Blessed Elizabeth of the Trinity.

DEVOTION TO CHRIST

Teresa considered joining the Sacred Heart Sisters, who were an educational order, but was overwhelmed by the need to devote her life to Christ. Her father was reluctant to give his permission when she told him she preferred to join an enclosed order, but he and the family did support her when, at 19, she became a noviciate with the Carmelite nuns.

The Carmelite convent in Los Andes was a rough building that lacked electricity and plumbing. Here, she took the vow of Victimhood, which meant that she was prepared to suffer for the Church and for sinners. Teresa's hours were spent deep in prayer, fasting, learning methods of contemplation, and recording and sharing her spiritual experiences in letters and a diary.

She was not quite 20 years old when she died of typhus at the convent, but her piety was regarded with great respect, and slowly, the power of her "hidden life" of devotion was revealed. A cultus grew around her memory and she was canonized by Pope John Paul II in 1993.

Left Personal messages for St Teresa of Los Andes cover a wall outside the church dedicated to her in Los Andes, Chile.

BERTILLA BOSCARDIN

BERTILLA WAS A SIMPLE PEASANT WOMAN WHO HAD BEEN BADLY TREATED AS A CHILD, BUT HER PATIENCE AND STAUNCH RELIGIOUS FAITH MADE HER A WONDERFUL NURSE.

KEY FACTS
Nun, nurse
DATES: *1888–1922*
BIRTH PLACE: *near Vicenza, Italy*
FEAST DAY: *20 October*

This saint lived a humble life, but those whom she cared for loved her, and miracles have been attributed to her intercession.

Maria Bertilla Boscardin was a peasant girl who joined the Sisters of St Dorothy in Vicenza in 1904. The other nuns, considering her dim-witted, used her as a kitchen and laundry maid until her profession in 1907, when she was sent to care for children with diphtheria at the hospital in Treviso.

During World War I, Vicenza was bombed, but Bertilla remained calm, intent only on saving her patients. When the hospital was moved away from the front line to Como, the military authorities praised her work. But again, her simplicity was misinterpreted, and she was put to work in the laundry. Bertilla never complained, but in 1919, the Superior-General of the order rescued her and placed her in charge of the children's isolation ward back at Treviso, where she nursed with compassion.

Bertilla died while undergoing surgery. Her family and some of her former patients were present at her canonization in 1961.

Above Bertilla Boscardin worked as a nurse in Treviso, where she cared for the sick with patience and sympathy.

GIUSEPPE MOSCATI

GIUSEPPE MOSCATI BELIEVED HIS SCIENTIFIC KNOWLEDGE AND CARE OF THE SICK WERE A WAY TO REVEAL THE GLORY OF GOD AND CONSIDERED HIS MEDICAL WORK TO BE A "SUBLIME MISSION".

KEY FACTS
Doctor of medicine
DATES: *1860–1927*
BIRTH PLACE: *Benevento, Italy*
FEAST DAY: *16 November*

Giuseppe Moscati came from a family brave in their faith. His father was a magistrate who had risked his livelihood, when he refused to deny Christianity during the anti-clerical control of Italy during the mid-19th century.

Giuseppe was a top medical student at the University of Naples, where he specialized in biochemistry. After qualifying, he began working with patients afflicted with syphilis at the Hospital for Incurables, Santa Maria del Populo.

Parallel to his hospital duties, Giuseppe conducted medical research and gave free care to the poor. This entailed visiting the swarming slums of Naples, often at night, to tend the sick. His scientific learning was underpinned by his faith, and he treated patients for spiritual as well as medical problems.

In 1911, he was appointed Chair of Physiology at Naples University, but success did not turn him from his prayers or his veneration of Mary, the Blessed Virgin. Neither did he neglect his charity work. Patients, priests and laymen appreciated the spiritual dimension he brought to medicine. He died peacefully in his home and was canonized in 1987.

Above Pilgrims touch the hand of the Giuseppe Moscati statue at Gesù Nuovo Church in Naples, Italy.

MARIA FAUSTINA KOWALSKA

MARIA FAUSTINA KOWALSKA WAS A HUMBLE LAY SISTER, BUT HER HEAVENLY VISIONS, HER OBEDIENCE AND HER DEEP DEVOTION TO GOD, RECORDED IN HER DIARIES, BROUGHT HER SAINTHOOD.

KEY FACTS
*Visionary
and Polish mystic*
DATES: *1905–38*
BIRTH PLACE: *Glogowiec, Poland*
FEAST DAY: *25 August*

Maria Faustina Kowalska offered her own suffering to God to make amends for her sins and the sins of others. Her inspiration came from a miracle described in John's Gospel: after Jesus had healed a man who had been an invalid for 38 years, he said to him, "Sin no more, lest a worse thing come unto thee." The man went away and told others that Jesus had made him well. Maria believed that with faith and virtue, sins would be forgiven, just as the faith of the invalid had banished his disability.

A LIFE GUIDED BY VISIONS

Born in Glogowiec, Poland, Maria was the third of ten children. She was certain that she had a vocation to the religious life, and in 1923,

Above Cracow, Poland, where Maria Faustina Kowalska spent the last few years of her life in contemplation and prayer while she fought off illness.

she had a vision of Christ that strengthened her conviction. In 1925, she joined the Congregation of Our Lady of Mercy in Warsaw as a lay sister.

She did not aim for high office, and nursed no ambition but, in humility and obedience, worked in the garden, the kitchen and as a porter. The compassion and patience she showed toward the poor who visited the convent impressed her fellow nuns.

DIVINE MERCY

Visions of Jesus were a frequent part of Maria's experience, and in one of these Christ is said to have asked her to keep a diary. In this, she began to record the spiritual guidance the visions brought her, primarily the message of the "Divine Mercy of God". Her diary was later published with the title *Divine Mercy in My Soul: The Diary of St Faustina*.

Her health was delicate, and in 1936 she was moved to a sanatorium in Cracow with suspected tuberculosis. Here, she was given her own cell, and in this privacy she was able to surrender herself to prayer and contemplation. Her last years were spent fighting for breath and in constant pain. She died in Cracow, still a young woman, in 1938, and was canonized by Pope John Paul II in 2000.

Left The canonization of Maria Faustina Kowalska by Pope John Paul II took place in front of 100,000 pilgrims in 2000.

MAXIMILIAN KOLBE

MAXIMILIAN KOLBE MADE THE ULTIMATE SACRIFICE, GIVING UP HIS LIFE FOR THE SAKE OF ANOTHER IN A GERMAN CONCENTRATION CAMP. HE IS KNOWN AS THE "MARTYR OF CHARITY".

KEY FACTS
Martyr
DATES: *1894–1941*
BIRTH PLACE: *near Lodz, Poland*
FEAST DAY: *14 August*

Maximilian Kolbe was the son of devout, patriotic Polish parents. After Maximilian entered the Franciscan Order in 1910, his parents separated and began living religious lives. His father was hanged by the Russian government in 1914, because he was fighting with the Polish Legion for Polish independence.

In 1912, Maximilian was sent to Cracow, then to Rome, where he studied philosophy, theology, physics and mathematics. After his ordination in Rome in 1919, he founded Franciscan communities dedicated to prayer and serving the poor at Niepokalanow, near Warsaw, and at Nagasaki in Japan. He was keen to revive the faith and started various religious publications in both Poland and Japan to accomplish this. He also took advantage of modern technology by installing a radio station at Niepokalanow.

HOUSING REFUGEES

When the Germans invaded Poland in 1939, Maximilian closed the Niepokalanow community and sent the priests home, anxious that they should not endanger themselves by joining the resistance. Heedless of his own safety, he and the remaining brothers housed 4,500 Polish refugees, of whom 1,500 were Jewish. Maximilian's various publications continued and included articles critical of the German invaders. In 1941, he and four brothers were arrested and taken to the Nazi concentration camp at Auschwitz in Poland.

***Above** An undated photograph of Maximilian Kolbe, the Franciscan priest who served, then gave up his life for fellow Poles in World War II.*

GIVING HIS LIFE

Maximilian had suffered tuberculosis most of his life, so he found his duties at the camp – carrying logs and moving the bodies of dead inmates – particularly hard. He applied himself to giving his fellow sufferers religious comfort, and somehow even managed to smuggle bread and wine inside the walls so that he could offer the Holy Eucharist.

One day, the inmates from Maximilian's hut were lined up and the wardens selected several men to die. This was a reprisal for a successful escape attempt. One of the chosen, a Polish sergeant named Francis Gajowniczek, cried out, "My poor wife! My poor children! What will they do?" Maximilian stepped forward and announced, "I wish to die for that man. I am old; he has a wife and children."

The swap was approved and the condemned men were locked into Cell 18 and left to starve. Maximilian comforted them, sang psalms and prayed in preparation for their deaths. After two weeks, he was the only man still conscious. He was killed by lethal injection in August 1941.

Sergeant Gajowniczek – who himself died at the age of 94 in 1995 – attended the canonization of St Maximilian Kolbe in 1982.

***Below** Francis Gajowniczek, the man saved by Maximilian Kolbe in 1941, is embraced by Pope John Paul II in St Peter's Square in 1982.*

KATHARINE DREXEL

KATHARINE DREXEL, MOTIVATED BY A PROFOUND FAITH, USED HER INHERITANCE TO IMPROVE THE SOCIAL AND RELIGIOUS WELFARE OF RACIAL MINORITIES AND DEPRIVED PEOPLES.

KEY FACTS
Founder
DATES: *1858–1955*
BIRTH PLACE: *Philadelphia,
USA*
FEAST DAY: *3 March*

Katharine Marie Drexel learnt the Christian virtue of charity from her stepmother, Emma Bouvier, who donated $20,000 a year to the welfare of the poor in Philadelphia. Another influence was Dr James O'Connor, a priest and family friend who campaigned for the just administration of Native Americans.

In 1878, Katharine "came out" in society, but she remained unmoved by the lavish circuit of balls and parties enjoyed by many of her peers. During a trip to Europe, she made a pilgrimage to the home of St Catherine of

Below A statue of Katharine Drexel in the National Shrine of the Immaculate Conception in Washington, D.C.

Above A painting of Katharine Drexel (artist and date unknown) shows her with some of the children she gave her life to serve.

Siena, and later confided to Dr O'Connor that she wished to become a nun.

By 1885, O'Connor, who had recently been appointed Bishop of Omaha, called on Katharine to help him resolve disputes between white and Native Americans in Dakota. On her return, she and her sisters, all wealthy women, founded the Drexel Chair of Moral Theology at Washington University (D.C.).

At an audience with Pope Leo XIII in 1887, she was encouraged by the pope to become a missionary. Taking his advice, and fulfilling her dream of a life dedicated to God, Katharine joined the Sisters of Mary in Pittsburgh.

AIDING MINORITIES

Katharine was determined to start a community devoted to helping ethnic minorities, and, in 1891, founded the Sisters of the Blessed

Sacrament. In 1894, the order's first school for Native American children, St Catherine Indian School, was built in Santa Fe, New Mexico.

She established schools, missions and hospitals in Boston, Chicago, New Orleans, New York, Texas and Tennessee, and her congregation trained nearly 200 teaching sisters and 80 lay teachers. She also founded the first university for African American students, Xavier University in New Orleans.

Katharine worked until she was disabled by illness (she suffered a severe heart attack in 1935). Thereafter, she continued to pray for, and advise her communities, who all knew her as "First Sister". She died in Philadelphia in 1955 at the age of 97. At her funeral, the pallbearers represented the groups she had helped – Native Americans, African Americans and European Americans.

Although Katharine focused on the welfare of racial minorities, her work extended to all the underprivileged. From the time she founded her order at the age of 33 until the end of her life, Katherine gave away a personal fortune of 20 million US dollars to the work of the Sisters of the Blessed Sacrament.

She also funded many convents, monasteries and chapels. Her congregation, which remains rooted in the welfare and education programmes she instituted, still has an important role within the Church. Katharine Drexel was canonized by Pope John Paul II in 2000.

FATHER GEORGE PRECA

FATHER GEORGE PRECA LOVED THE GOSPELS, WHICH HE CALLED "THE VOICE OF THE BELOVED". A HUMBLE MAN, HE DEVOTED HIS LIFE TO TEACHING THE DEPRIVED AND UNEDUCATED.

KEY FACTS
Founder
DATES: *1880–1962*
BIRTH PLACE: *Valletta, Malta*
FEAST DAY: *9 May*

The young George Preca was cured of an illness after prayers of intercession to St Joseph. Throughout his life, George heard heavenly voices and had visions, and these spiritual experiences gave him a powerful sense of his mission on earth. He was inspired, too, by the words of Jesus, "Blessed are the meek, for they shall inherit the earth" (Matthew 5:5).

MALTESE MISSION

After he was ordained in 1906, George began to seek out ordinary working people, and he set up a mission on the waterfront of Valletta, Malta. In 1907, he founded a community that came to be called the Society of Christian Doctrine. This order of laymen and women pursued mission work throughout Malta, and Father George sent them forth with the hope that "the world would follow the gospel". These missions organized daily sessions of prayer and discussion, and taught children the Catechism.

However, the Church in Malta was displeased with George's inclusion of lay people in the Church hierarchy and his use of female missionaries. They tried to shut down the order, but encountered such uproar from believers and other priests that Father George was eventually reinstated, and the Society of Christian Doctrine was given approval in 1932. During the controversy, Father George cautioned his followers to quell their anger and forgive those who taunted them.

***Above** Pope John Paul II prays at the tomb of Father George Preca in Hamrun, Malta, in 2001.*

***Below** The cityscape of Valletta, Malta, the birthplace of Father George Preca.*

A HOLY, HUMBLE MAN

The Maltese admired Father George as a gentle, sympathetic confessor, and as a priest who welcomed the laity into the rituals of the Church. He was regarded as a holy man and saw a vision of the boy Jesus, which, he reported, brought him a sense of great spiritual sweetness. Others claimed he had cured their physical ailments.

The society's reputation spread, and it now has missions in Albania, Australia, Kenya, Peru and Sudan. Pope Pius XII made Father George a Monsignor of the Church, but the honour embarrassed him, and he dropped the title after the pope's death.

Father George Preca died at Santa Venera, Malta, in 1962, and his relics lie in Blata I-Badja. Prayers for his intercession have been known to cure the sick. He was canonized in 2007 by Pope Benedict XVI.

PADRE PIO

THE HUMBLE CAPUCHIN MONK, NOW BEST KNOWN AS PADRE PIO, MODESTLY TRIED TO HIDE THE MARKS OF HIS STIGMATA, SAYING, "I ONLY WANT TO BE A POOR FRIAR WHO PRAYS".

KEY FACTS
Stigmatist
DATES: *1887–1968*
BIRTH PLACE: *near Naples, Italy*
FEAST DAY: *23 September*

St Pius of Pietrelcina, better known as Padre Pio, first knew he belonged to God at the age of five. Throughout his childhood, he experienced visions and spoke with Jesus and Mary. He joined the Capuchin Order and was ordained at the friary of San Giovanni Rotondo, Pietrelcina in 1910.

RECEIVING THE STIGMATA

In 1918, he became "aware that my hands, feet and side were pierced and were dripping with blood". He had received stigmata, but he covered the wounds and tried unsuccessfully to hide them.

Padre Pio may have been awed, even frightened, by this gift of holy marks, but he could not have anticipated the antagonism he met within the Church. When his secret was revealed, other churchmen claimed he was a fake and accused him of sexual licence, but

Above Padre Pio as depicted on the front of Italian magazine La Domenica del Corriere *in 1956.*

Below A friar bends over the coffin of Padre Pio. During his lifetime Pio was both revered and reviled. The controversy continued after his death in 1968.

believers crowded the friary, seeking blessings and forgiveness from him. In 1923, the Church placed increasingly severe restrictions on Padre Pio until he was virtually locked away and only allowed to take Mass in private. After Pope Pius XII lifted all these restrictions in 1933, life became easier for Padre Pio, but spiteful attacks from other clergy continued. True to Christ's teachings, Padre Pio remained meek and dedicated, despite slander and injustice.

MAN OF PRAYER

The Capuchins had built, in the friary grounds, a House for the Relief of Suffering, a place that was a hospital, hospice and retreat directed toward families in need. Pius XII encouraged Padre Pio to pray for the hospital. The saint spent long hours praying and meditating on the Way of the Cross, saying, "In books we seek God, in prayer we meet him."

In 1959, he began regular broadcasts on national radio, his sermons reinforcing his belief that "Prayer is the best weapon we possess, the key that opens the heart of God." His example inspired prayer groups across the world and these continue today.

Padre Pio wore mittens to hide the stigmata on his hands, and remained a humble friar, who spent all his life in his friary and died there, yet more than 100,000 people attended his funeral. A mother claimed a miracle cure of her child's meningitis after prayers to Padre Pio, who was canonized in 2002.

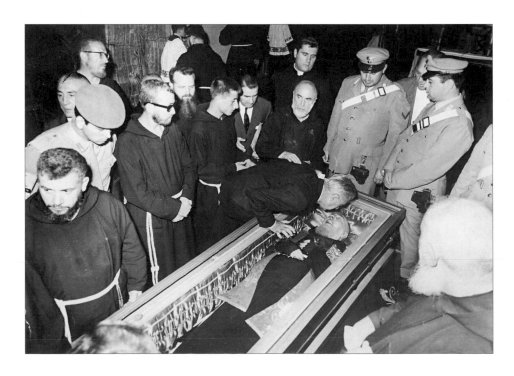

INDEX

Above Tobias and the angel.